D0887516

CRISIS

LEADERSHIP

Center for
Creative
Leadership®

The Center for Creative Leadership is an international, nonprofit educational institution founded in 1970 to advance the understanding, practice, and development of leadership for the benefit of society worldwide. As a part of this mission, it publishes books and reports that aim to contribute to a general process of inquiry and understanding in which ideas related to leadership are raised, exchanged, and evaluated. The ideas presented in its publications are those of the author or authors.

CENTER FOR CREATIVE LEADERSHIP

WWW.CCL.ORG

Gene Klann

CRISIS
LEADERSHIP

Using Military Lessons,
Organizational Experiences, and
the Power of Influence to Lessen
the Impact of Chaos on the
People You Lead

CENTER FOR CREATIVE LEADERSHIP
Greensboro, North Carolina

CCL Stock No. 185
© 2003 Center for Creative Leadership

Published by CCL Press
Martin Wilcox, Director of Publications
Peter Scisco, Editor, CCL Press
Joanne Ferguson, Production Editor

Cover design by Joanne Ferguson

Library of Congress Cataloging-in-Publication Data

Klann, Gene.
    Crisis leadership : using military lessons, organizational experiences, and the power of influence to lessen the impact of chaos on the people you lead / Gene Klann.
        p. cm.
    Includes bibliographical references.
    ISBN 978-1-932973-70-9 (print) — ISBN 978-1-932973-26-6 (ebook)
    1. Leadership. 2. Crisis management. I. Title.

HD57.7.K547 2003
658.4'092—dc21
                                                        2003046010

CONTENTS

PROLOGUE

December 1944. The Second World War is grinding to what appears to be an inevitable conclusion. Almost all of the Allied commanders in the European theatre of operations believe that the German Army is on the verge of collapse. But on December 16 the Germans launch a surprise attack. Several armored and infantry divisions strike the Allied lines and threaten to break through to the harbor of Antwerp, to cut off some Allied forces in Holland and Belgium, while surrounding others.

At the time of the attack, not all of the Allied commanders were convinced that the German Army stood on the brink of defeat. Among them was George S. Patton Jr. Intelligence reports that the Germans were massing for a major attack did not pass Patton's command unnoticed or without reflection. Patton directed his staff to prepare a response just in case—he paid attention to the signs of an impending crisis, took them seriously, and made preparations to meet it head on. When General Eisenhower asked his subordinate leaders what they could do to meet this emergency, Patton declared he would lead three of his divisions out of the front line, turn them north, travel 120 miles on icy roads in the middle of winter, and attack the Germans. And, he said, he would do it in 72 hours. . . .

(To be continued)

PREFACE

The idea to write this book was not inspired by the terrorist acts of September 11, 2001. I did not write it to confirm or critique the leaders involved in the 9/11 crisis. However, that event certainly underscored my desire to put these ideas about crisis leadership into a book that would be applicable across a large range of traumatic situations. My personal interest in the subject of crisis leadership, coupled with the almost daily news reports of both natural and man-made crises, encouraged me to share my experiences, research, and understanding of what it takes to lead during such times.

There are many books written about crisis management, but few focus on crisis leadership. Managing a crisis and providing leadership in a crisis are not the same thing, although each addresses different aspects of a difficult situation. I would differentiate the two by saying that crisis management relates mainly to operational issues, while crisis leadership principally deals with how leaders handle the human responses to a crisis, including their own. We all have natural behavioral responses to crisis situations based on our needs and emotions. We may not be conscious of this, but our behaviors send messages to others about our underlying needs and emotions. It is within this set of behaviors that we find the core of crisis leadership.

I write about leading in difficult situations from the vantage point of more than 25 years of crisis leadership training and experience during a career as an active duty officer in the United States Army. This includes decorated service as an infantry company advisor in the Vietnam War and as a battalion commander of 600 paratroopers during the Gulf War. My contention, which I believe is shared by many others, is that the United States military (and particularly its army) ranks among the best organizations in the world for crisis leadership planning, training, research, and experience. Many of the notions I share in this book come from the army's vast database in the areas of crisis leadership and crisis planning, which documents best practices and failed experiences of soldiers in combat, a grueling crisis by anyone's definition.

But this book is not just a litany of the army way of leadership, useful only to those few people who must lead in the most harrowing situations. Leaders in the private sector can readily adopt many of the army's crisis leadership lessons. But what is the argument for civilian leaders' adopting such tactics? The answer lies in the army's dramatic and well-documented post–Vietnam change in leadership philosophy, which brought about one of the most successful organizational transformations in recent history. Gone is the popular Hollywood and news media image of the yelling, abusive, and irrational military leader. The combination of the military's high-tech equipment, its growing participation in international missions, and its extremely diverse volunteer force has created a very different mid- and upper-level army leader.

The average army officer's experience and training with crisis situations is extensive. The necessity of training for and the experience of leading in high-stress situations has resulted in the officer having a high degree of flexibility, a calm and coolness under fire (literally), a degree of comfort in making quick decisions, and an appreciation for teamwork. These are leaders who have had several global assignments, can speak more than one language, are educated beyond their civilian counterparts, and, even as junior leaders, have had responsibilities that equal those of mid-level and some upper-level corporate leaders. This is not profit-and-loss responsibility, but life-and-death responsibility. For these reasons alone, there is much that the civilian leader can learn from the army's leadership renaissance.

I wish to extend special recognition to a number of individuals whose support, encouragement, and cooperation made this work possible. At the top of the list is my wife, Kathy, who is my best friend as well as my most trusted confidante, critic, and counselor. I also want to recognize my mentor, Dr. Hubert Dethier, who shared with me the challenge, excitement, and rewards of sound scholarship. Thanks also go to my friend Dr. Claude Ragan, who assisted in my understanding of the relationships between needs, emotions, feelings, and behaviors.

I would also like to express my sincere appreciation to those colleagues who reviewed this work and offered comments, suggestions, ideas, and criticisms. A special thanks must go to Peter Scisco whose accomplished editing skills made this book a reality.

INTRODUCTION

Nothing tests a leader like a crisis. There is an element of the leader's deepest character that is revealed during highly charged, dramatic events. A crisis can quickly expose a leader's hidden strengths and core weaknesses. It can show the world if the leader has what it takes to function effectively when the heat is on. Will the leader address the crisis head-on, take those actions needed to fix it, and, if appropriate, take responsibility for the crisis? Will the leader freeze, or worse, claim to be a victim and pass off the responsibility to others? What can and should a leader do to find out what went wrong and to ensure it doesn't happen again?

This book is a brief but sincere attempt to address those kinds of questions. It's not the definitive work on crisis leadership, nor is it a technical manual of crisis procedures. It approaches its subject by describing how a leader can handle the human side of a crisis and examining what leaders can do to effectively deal with the emotions, behaviors, and attitudes of the people involved in or facing a crisis. It defines a crisis and argues for a style of leadership that is particularly effective during a time of crisis. This book also includes information about human nature that is essential for leaders to understand if they are to be effective in a crisis situation.

At its center, this book deals with three key themes of crisis leadership and their impact on helping people and organizations through perilous times. These themes—communication, clarity of vision and values, and caring relationships—are certainly important to leaders in normal operations, but their importance is magnified during a crisis. By paying attention to these themes, leaders can hope to increase their understanding of practices that handle the human dimension of a crisis. The result is a leader more prepared to contain the crisis, regain control of the situation, ensure the minimum amount of damage is done to the organization, and effectively prevent, defuse, and reduce the duration of these extremely difficult leadership situations.

Practicing leaders all along the organizational chain can find many of the ideas presented here useful, not just for their daily managerial tasks but also for their personal leadership development. As a means to understanding these leadership issues, readers can use this book to assess their strengths and weaknesses, learn new competencies, and prepare for events that are as unpredictable as they are unavoidable.

The anxiety, insecurity, and confusion that a crisis generates are huge challenges for civilian leaders. They must be prepared to provide leadership not only to those in their organization, but also to those in the greater orbit of their influence: clients and customers, the surrounding community, stockholders, suppliers, vendors, local government, concerned organizations, activist groups, and the media. And, of course, leaders must also lead themselves. They must deal with their own emotions and needs a crisis triggers. For some leaders, this may be the biggest challenge of all.

1
WHAT IS CRISIS?

Crises have no borders or boundaries. They can happen anytime, anywhere, and to any organization—profit, not-for-profit, public, or private. The interconnectedness of the global economy and its political realities can magnify the ripple effect of any single crisis, making it a common feature of corporate life. A crisis affecting one organization can, among other things, cause layoffs and closings among that organization's suppliers, customers, and partners; bring about a loss of investor confidence that can cause a dip in the stock market; and even bring about environmental damage and psychological angst. The financial implosion that bankrupted the U.S.-based energy-trading company Enron in the fall and winter of 2001, for example, also sparked a financial crisis at Arthur Andersen, a consulting and auditing services firm. The publicity surrounding the subsequent investigation into both companies led investors to question financial records at scores of other publicly traded companies, which in turn suffered their own crises—some more damaging than the Enron debacle.

Because of their unpredictable nature and their accompanying ripple effect, crisis situations are unlikely to leave any organization untouched forever. Leaders should not pretend otherwise. They can realistically count on facing some kind of organizational crisis at some point during their careers. Such a crisis will negatively affect people in an organization, which is often the most pernicious and difficult challenge leaders face in dealing with a crisis. But they can act to reduce the probability of a crisis reoccurring, reduce the duration of a crisis, and soften the negative impact by addressing the human element of a crisis before, during, and after it occurs.

The Panic Button

A crisis is generally characterized by a high degree of instability and carries the potential for extremely negative results that can endanger the continuity of the organization. It's a key moment or critical period that brings both surprise and dramatic change. In this way a crisis can be described as a turning point in the affairs of an individual or an organization. It's significant because the consequences of the situation will be decisive in determining the future of that individual or organization. The word itself originates from the Greek krisis, which means "to sift or separate." A crisis has the potential to divide an organization's past from its future, to replace security with insecurity, and to separate effective leaders from ineffective ones. A crisis also has the potential to swap routine for creativity and to shift an organization from "business as usual" into significant change.

Many crises are generated by an emergency—a sudden condition or state of affairs that calls for immediate action. The crisis itself includes the emergency that served as its catalyst. The situation may be further aggravated by relentless media scrutiny, a restless and information-hungry workforce, and advanced technologies that are never 100 percent reliable. Think about the kinds of emergencies reported daily in the newspaper or on TV and how such emergencies lead to crisis situations.

- product failure/recall
- hostile takeover
- financial catastrophe
- hazardous material spill
- toxic chemical release/leak
- lawsuit
- crash or derailment
- natural disaster

- employee sabotage/violence
- strike/boycott
- executive scandal/defection
- act of war
- industrial accident
- succession at the top

Although no two crises are ever the same, they share some common traits. For example, a crisis isn't usually expected or planned for. It generally comes as a bombshell that frightens and stuns those on whom it falls. There may have been signs and indications of impending difficulties, but in the flow of daily operations they were ignored, placed on the back burner, or wished away. The element of shock and even terror can be sharp and devastating if the crisis has an element of physical danger, if the crisis causes a death or serious injury, or if the crisis results in the destruction of property (for example, one's office or place of work). For these reasons a crisis can exert a high impact on human needs, emotions, and behaviors.

In defining a crisis it's helpful to think about the seriousness of the threat. The amount of impact a crisis will have on an organization's leadership, workers, and stakeholders often depends on its severity. Along these lines, a useful breakdown of a crisis might place it at one of three levels of severity.

Level 1 crisis. In this situation the organization will be publicly embarrassed and mission success is threatened. Common examples of this level of crisis include sexual harassment charges brought against a key leader of the organization; an insensitive or racially charged statement by a company leader; or an overt action taken by the organization that damages the environment, places profit over public welfare, or is viewed as unethical, politically incorrect, or socially irresponsible. A specific case in point is the racial discrimination lawsuit filed against Texaco, an American oil company. African Americans had been complaining for years about discrimination in hiring and promotions. In 1996 a taped conversation among four senior white Texaco executives came to light and revealed vile and offensive attitudes toward African Americans employed at the company. A class-action lawsuit demanded $520 million in damages; Texaco settled out of court for $176 million and drew the ire and a boycott from African Americans across the country.

Level 2 crisis. At this level a situation exists in which there is personal injury, some property loss, possible loss of life, potential for serious damage to the company's reputation, or a combination of these and similar items. An example of a level 2 crisis can be found at Johnson & Johnson. In the fall of 1982 seven people died in the Chicago area from taking cyanide-laced Tylenol (one of the company's premiere products). Public relations experts consider the company's handling of the crisis as one of the best examples of crisis leadership and corporate communications in the history of American business. Johnson & Johnson placed customer safety over corporate profits by immediately recalling $10 million worth of Tylenol from store shelves and warehouses, stopping both production and advertising of the product, cooperating with the media to inform the public of the problem, and offering a $100,000 reward for information leading to the killer's capture. In 1983 the company reintroduced Tylenol with tamper resistant packaging. Because of the socially responsible manner in which the organization handled the crisis, confidence was regained and Tylenol's market share was virtually restored to where it was prior to the crisis.

Level 3 crisis. This level defines a situation in which there is loss of life, significant property damage, a perceived threat to the survival of the company, or a combination of these and similar items. An example of a level 3 crisis is the accounting scandal at the Enron Corporation. The Houston-based organization inflated its profits and disguised its financial difficulties, and its leaders funneled millions into their own pockets. The company's bankruptcy, in December 2001, produced billions of dollars of shareholder losses, thousands of job losses, and a near wipeout of employee 401(k) assets. Key Enron leaders were investigated for fraud and other financial abuses (one committed suicide), and Enron's attempt at reorganizing has been inhibited by dozens of lawsuits filed by investors, pension funds, and lenders. The value of Enron's stock was erased, and it has since been removed from the New York Stock Exchange. The firm of Arthur Andersen, whose job it was to ensure investors could rely on Enron's financial statements, was convicted of obstruction of justice for the shredding of Enron's financial documents during a Securities and Exchange Commission

Crisis Is Emotional Chaos

The military's single peacetime focus is preparing for combat, the ultimate crisis situation because it involves life and death. A major element of the military's training teaches soldiers how to deal with the range of emotions they will experience before, during, and after combat. These emotions generally include horror, apprehension, grief, rage, revenge, loneliness, sadness, repulsion, vigilance, anguish, and guilt. Military leaders know these emotions will be experienced and must be controlled or the soldiers will not be able to function on the battlefield.

Combat leaders must learn to deal with their own emotions as well as with the emotions of the soldiers under their charge. This is the same challenge civilian leaders face during a crisis, and they can expect the same kinds of emotional chaos to flow over the people in their organization and themselves.

investigation. As a result of their part in the Enron scandal, many key Arthur Andersen employees have either left or been laid off. Like Enron, the company also faces the possibility of staggering liability claims. The firm no longer performs auditing work.

Crisis also has the tendency to bring a high degree of chaos and confusion into an organization. Typically, there is a lack of information precisely when virtually everyone in the organization has a huge emotional need for it. Those involved have a need to know and understand what happened, why it happened, and how it will impact their futures. Ambiguity is especially potent.

High-stress situations, such as a crisis, can move usually rational people away from sense and reason. In addition to those already listed (see "Crisis Is Emotional Chaos" on page 7), common emotions arising in crisis situations include fear, anger, anxiety, sorrow, surprise, shock, disgust, love, and the desire for revenge. These emotions can trigger positive or negative behaviors (the emotions themselves are not positive or negative, but the behaviors they trigger can be). People in a crisis can act with compassion, self-sacrifice, and courage, or they can display selfishness, cowardice, and greed. The potential for conflict and illogical behavior can be great. Previously dysfunctional behavior has the potential to become even more dysfunctional during a crisis. For those emotionally impacted by the crisis, even the simplest tasks can become difficult to perform. It is in this chaotic, ambiguous, and highly charged emotional environment—one rife with the human element—that leaders must lead, and lead well.

Opportunity or Chaos?

Effective crisis leadership boils down to responding to the human needs, emotions, and behaviors caused by the crisis. Effective leaders respond to those emotional needs as those needs are perceived by those experiencing the crisis, not just to their personal

Learning from the Crisis Experience
For more than 15 years, the Center for Creative Leadership (CCL) has researched the key events that have shaped the careers and lives of executives. That research indicates that hardships, such as those experienced during a crisis, can result in significant learning. In fact, 34 percent of the hundreds of managers CCL has interviewed indicated that their greatest learning occurred from hardships, which included leading in a crisis situation. Because people can learn from hardships, a crisis can develop personal and organizational leadership capacity by providing opportunities such as the following:

- hardships cause individuals and organizations to examine what is important, to further define or redefine their core values;
- crises renew individuals and organizations by getting rid of the old and bringing in the new;
- crises bring out courage, honor, selflessness, loyalty, and many other positive behaviors;
- individuals leading or otherwise involved in the crisis learn lessons about their own strength of character and how much adversity they can take;
- handling a crisis promotes confidence and personal growth;
- what survives the crisis emerges better and stronger than before—it's tempered by the hardship;
- a crisis can create bonding and a keen sense of camaraderie and community among employees through the power of a shared experience.

perception of what those emotional needs are, might be, or should be. The crisis will affect employee morale, attitudes, productivity, ability to focus, stress levels, relationships, and more. People are more apt to follow a leader who is reassuring and who can meet their primary needs—those needs they least want to give up.

Effective crisis leadership can rescue an organization from chaos and deliver opportunities where before there were only disadvantages. Organizations that successfully handle crisis situations can come out of them stronger and with greater employee, customer, and community loyalty than existed prior to the crisis. Leaders must look deep into the crisis for such opportunities that not only benefit the organization but also raise the potential for individual achievement among the organization's employees. In their search, they should look to human elements—the emotions, the behaviors, and the reactions that affect and are affected by the crisis and can influence its outcome.

2
WHAT IS CRISIS LEADERSHIP?

Leading in a crisis can be extremely difficult and challenging. Managers who have led in such circumstances describe the experience as highly developmental—a benchmark in their professional careers. But what does effective leadership during a crisis look like? There may be as many descriptions of leadership, and crisis leadership, as there are executive coaches and management gurus. In some of its educational activities, CCL has described leadership as a process of influence in which managers interact with direct reports and others in the organization in collective pursuit of a common goal. Given the emotionally volatile environment that surrounds a crisis situation, and that can contribute to ineffective or even counterproductive behavior, a useful working definition of crisis leadership may simply be this ability to influence others.

A Definition of Leadership

Influence is the ability to persuade, convince, motivate, inspire, and judiciously use power to affect others in a positive way. Generally speaking, it's not the kind of authority that comes from leveraging title, position, or regulations. But exactly how is this different from other methods of leadership that managers carry out every single day? After all, the ability to influence others is an important part of leadership in good circumstances as well as bad. The power of influence would seem to be a useful leadership skill no matter what the style of the individual leader (some managers are more inclusive than others and some are more autocratic, for example, in the way they approach their work). The difference lies not in the importance of influence as a leadership capacity but rather in the particular context of crisis itself, an emotional cauldron that distills the components of influence into a potent concentrate of three key elements: communication, clarity of vision and values, and caring. Crisis leadership is a special case in which these specific tools of influence perform a critical role. In a crisis, timelines are more critical. There isn't as much time for reflection. Rapid decision making and a higher call to action become the norm.

In his book *Leadership in Organizations,* Gary Yukl lists several influencing tactics that people commonly use. Among these he includes ingratiation, exchange (quid pro quo), coalition, inspirational and personal appeals, consultation, legitimizing, and pressure. His description of these tactics suggests that managers can categorize them (and others can perceive them) as either positive or negative in their practice. For example, using pressure and micromanagement to achieve results (such as checking frequently on a direct report's progress with a specific assignment) can have a negative impact during the best of times and especially during a crisis. On the other hand, personal appeals based on a legitimate relationship between managers and direct reports (one constructed not just on rank and position but on a common interest and vision) can also bring results and are more effective during a crisis.

All of these general influencing tactics are useful for a leader before, during, and after a crisis. Along with these tactics are personal influencing methods that leaders can practice and that can also be highly effective during a crisis. These personal methods can be grouped into skills, traits, and perspectives. Leaders can develop skills through training and through experiences like problem solving, decision making, and conflict resolution. Leaders can fine-tune traits (individual characteristics) by paying attention to such areas as integrity, courage, and risk taking. Perspectives, which include the attitudes and points of view held toward leadership (if leaders take care of their direct reports they don't have to worry about accomplishing the mission, for example), can be fuel for further reflection and learning in an effort to bolster leadership competence and confidence—things sorely needed in times of crisis.

Each skill, trait, and perspective is a useful tool for leading during a crisis. But they are even more effective when integrated into a single crisis leadership strategy. Consider how the following skills, traits, and perspectives might add to a leader's ability to get results through others even during times of crisis. Of the eight listed here (this list isn't exhaustive; many more skills, traits, and perspectives have an effect on the leader's ability to influence), the first three are most crucial—the distilled essence from the cauldron—to crisis leadership. Examples of the skills, traits, and perspectives drawn from civilian and military history illustrate how these capabilities form crisis leadership.

Communication. A well-honed communication strategy is essential and critical to any organization before, during, and after a crisis situation. But there are also personal communication skills leaders can sharpen to make themselves more effective in those situations. Those skills include clear and articulate verbal expression that takes into account tone of voice, choice of words, and tempo of speech. Another is careful listening that involves appropriate eye contact, responsive gestures (such as saying "OK" or "sure"), not interrupting, and repeating key points to ensure understanding. Personal communication skills related to appropriate body language and a clear, concise, and straight-forward writing style are also helpful during a crisis. Consider, for example, the monumental task faced by Winston Churchill during World War II. He was able to maintain and even boost the morale of the British people during the London Blitz largely through his oratory skills. His distinctive voice, message of hope, and spirit of defiance became a rallying point in Britain's fight against Nazism. His communicating met a great emotional need in the British people, who wanted to know that things were going to be fine regardless of how bad the situation appeared.

Clarity of vision and values. Having a clear vision and value system (either personal or passed down from the organization) that can be communicated so direct reports understand it, feel ownership of it, and endorse it is a powerful influencing tool, before, during, and after a crisis. But clarity of vision is only effective if it is associated with a set of values that clarify what is important to the organization and what isn't. During a crisis the leader can leverage a credible vision and value system and use both as a rallying point and as a way to provide stability to employees who are rocked by events. Consider the story of the Chrysler Corporation, which was in a deep financial crisis when Lee Iacocca was hired as its CEO in 1979. That year, Chrysler announced a third-quarter loss of $160 million, the worst deficit in its history. But in the midst of this crisis Iacocca had a positive vision for Chrysler that never wavered. His vision for the corporation's recovery was so strong and so clear that he convinced several of his former executives at Ford to join him; he convinced still others to come out of retirement and be part of his team; he made many management changes that sharply improved the morale of his embattled workforce; and, finally, against vigorous opposition, he convinced the United States federal government to give him a $1.5 billion loan guarantee. Despite temporary setbacks, his vision for the organization remained positive and focused. In 1982, three years after Iacocca took over, Chrysler made a small profit. In 1983 it made close to $1 billion. The company paid off the entire government-guaranteed loan seven years before it was due. As a result, Iacocca became an industrial folk hero and a capitalist icon. Such is the impact of a leader whose vision is clear and unwavering in a crisis situation.

Caring. A sincere interest and genuine concern for others goes a long way toward meeting the emotional needs of people experiencing a crisis. Just consider what it is like to be on the receiving end of an inconsiderate or uncaring person. When normal, emotionally healthy people are treated with respect, dignity, approval, appreciation, attention, significance, value, and trust, they will generally respond in kind. Take the example of Aaron Feuerstein, the CEO of Malden Mills of Lawrence, Massachusetts. When a fire burned his production plant to the ground on December 11, 1995, Feuerstein declared in the parking lot during the fire that "this is not the end." He then spent millions of dollars keeping all 3,000 employees on the payroll and with full benefits for over three months. He had the plant rebuilt, and when his people went back to work, he saw the results of his caring attitude. Before the fire, the plant had been producing 130,000 yards of fabric a week. A few weeks after reopening the plant, production was up to 230,000 yards. Because of the manner in which Feuerstein had taken care of the employees during the crisis, they put their creativity and innovative skills into full gear. They indicated they were willing to work 25 hours a day to support Mr. Feuerstein. This degree of loyalty and support is a very usual response, not an aberration, when employees see clear evidence that their leaders really do care about them.

Personal example. All of us have a tendency to mimic the behavior of people whom we respect, regardless of their official position. Effective leaders leverage this tendency. All leaders would benefit from becoming more aware of the significant impact their words and actions have on others. Soliciting feedback from others (not during a crisis but during normal times) is an excellent way to assess how others perceive and respond to the example you set. For an inspiring story of personal example, look to the actions of

French General Francois Kellermann during the 1792 Battle of Valmy. Under heavy Prussian artillery fire, the forces commanded by Kellermann were beginning to waver and leave their guns. In reaction to this crisis, the 57-year-old Kellermann posted himself at the front rank of the infantry battalion most likely to receive the full force of the Prussian ground attack. He rallied the men of that battalion to be strong and to stand with him. His personal example of bravery, selflessness, and patriotism became contagious and spread along the entire French front line. With shouts of "Vive la Nation" rising from its ranks, the French line held, the Prussian attack was thwarted, and the French won a major victory. Personal example, from an individual leader, carries great force in a crisis situation.

Character. Synonymous with integrity, this trait of conscious moral behavior defines who you are when no one is watching. At a minimum, character implies telling the truth, being consistent in word and deed, treating people with dignity, avoiding actions that even hint at impropriety, and exercising self-control in the areas of morality and self-indulgence. Your direct reports will likely tolerate honest mistakes, but may find major moral lapses harder to deal with, especially if they cause layoffs or financial insecurity (pension plan losses, for example). These lapses can have a lasting negative impact on your reputation, erode your ability to lead, and increase the emotional impact of a crisis. Although not a familiar name anymore in the business titles stacked at the local bookstore, the common theme of nineteenth-century American author Horatio Alger was that to be successful in business one must be a person of character. If the leader did what was right, then things would turn out just fine. For Alger, character was more important than one's social background, education, or skills because a failure or gap in character would negate one's other positive characteristics and result in certain failure. In each of Alger's books (more than 50) the leader was faced with a crisis that could only be successfully resolved by an action or decision of high character. Alger's writings emphasizing character influenced millions, especially those American business leaders who forged the American Industrial Revolution.

Competence. That leaders should be technically capable of handling their positions is obvious almost to the point that it needs not be mentioned. No amount of personality, political skills, or cracker-barrel wit can disguise or overcome a deficit in basic technical and managerial competence. And almost nothing can multiply employee anxieties and reduce confidence more during a crisis than a leader who is perceived to be marginally competent. Competent leaders instill confidence and remove doubt and fear. Leaders can bolster their strengths and shore up weaknesses by continuously assessing their performance to ensure they have no glaring developmental needs or experiential shortcomings that hinder them from doing their job well in normal circumstances (those hindrances only magnify during a crisis). Developmental activities such as reading professional books and magazines (everything from biographies to expert discussions of contemporary management subjects), attending continuing education courses and executive training, and taking high-risk, high-payoff assignments are all ways in which leaders can build and maintain competence.

As a model of competence in a leadership role, it's difficult to improve upon the record of General Colin Powell. While serving from 1989 to 1993 as the chairman of the Joint Chiefs of Staff, the highest leadership position in the U.S. armed forces, he was faced with two crises: the invasion of Panama and, later, the liberation of Kuwait. As a direct result of his unusually high level of professional competence, both of these crisis situations were successfully dealt with swiftly and with a minimal loss of life and equipment. General Powell learned the lessons of crisis situations from his extensive studies of warfare as well as from his personal experiences in the Vietnam War. He effectively communicated his competence during numerous nationwide television briefings during both of these crises. His professional skills increased the public's confidence in the military and did much to increase national support and defuse public anxiety during both of those military operations.

Courage. It takes a high measure of courage to tell the truth under difficult circumstances, to make hard decisions, to answer tough questions, to face the unhappy crowd, and to accept responsibility. But these are the things asked of leaders when a crisis occurs. Your direct reports will want to know that you will go to bat for them and do the right thing regardless of the consequences or the political environment. Given the leadership failures and scandals among a few corporate giants during 2001 and 2002, courage is not always a common trait among senior leaders. A leader without courage courts disaster when a crisis strikes. To build a storehouse of personal courage, leaders can first develop a clear code of personal values, ethics, and standards. They can then relate each situation or decision to this code and follow their conscience to do what is right under the circumstances. This sounds simple, but it is one of the most difficult things for many leaders to do because of their overriding fear of negative consequences that might affect their reputation, security, and future.

Courage was on display in December 1984 when a chemical release at the Union Carbide insecticide plant in Bhopal, India, killed 3,800 people and disabled more than 11,000 (final figures from a reporting panel created by the Indian government). The catastrophe occurred on a Monday morning. Union Carbide CEO Warren M. Anderson flew to India on Tuesday. He was arrested on arrival and directed to leave the country. Despite his being rebuffed by Indian authorities, Anderson's example demonstrates that senior leaders should have the courage to travel to the site of the crisis despite the almost guaranteed negative response they will receive.

Decisiveness. During a crisis, even a wrong decision that promotes action is better than doing nothing. Influential decision making means gathering information and getting input as soon as possible, knowing that all the information needed to make the decision isn't available, accepting that there are risks involved, getting recommendations from others, listening to gut feelings, and making the decision because it needs to be made. During World War II, General of the Army Dwight D. Eisenhower's original plan for the D day invasion of Normandy included a drop of three airborne divisions onto the Cherbourg Peninsula. Their mission was to provide security for the Allies' amphibious landing forces. Eisenhower's senior air advisor, British Air Marshal Trafford Leigh-Mallory, opposed the airborne drop because he felt it was unnecessary and would result in over 50 percent casualties. He further believed the entire D day mission could fail because of these excessive losses. Eisenhower asked the air marshal to put his arguments opposing the airborne assault in writing. Once received, he studied the arguments, considered the counterarguments, determined that the risks were not as great as Leigh-Mallory had indicated, and decided to go with the airborne drop. He advised Leigh-Mallory of his decision and his reasoning. After the airborne assault succeeded, Leigh-Mallory admitted he had been wrong and congratulated Eisenhower on his decision. The lesson in this example is that in a crisis, leaders will be required to make many difficult and high-impact decisions, decisions they cannot shy away from, that may not be popular, and that will in many cases be counter to the advice of their senior staff. All of these decisions come with the mantle of leadership and are generally amplified in a crisis situation.

There are many other skills, traits, and perspectives that leaders can develop and sharpen to enhance their personal influence so that it's more effective during routine operations and during a crisis. Some obvious examples include being adaptable to change, promoting rewards and recognition, maintaining consistency and fairness in discipline, being enthusiastic and optimistic, keeping a sense of humor, endorsing a professional development process for employees, and leveraging strengths that a crisis may demand (such as fluency in a second language or extraordinary computer skills).

Leadership's Role in a Crisis

Ideally, all of us would balance our intellectual, physical, spiritual, and emotional lives all of the time. But that's a difficult job, particularly when a crisis creates an imbalance and tips the scale toward the emotional end. This creates a special challenge for managers who must provide leadership to those who are in a state of emotional turmoil.

Occupying a designated leadership position isn't the same thing as being a leader, doesn't provide leadership on its own, and doesn't prove that the person in that position has the skills or knowledge to be an effective leader. There is a significant difference between being a successful leader because specific numbers were achieved and being an effective leader because the numbers were achieved and the continuing support of direct reports is evident. Leaders who view themselves as successful because of position, salary, or longevity, but leave a high body count of former employees bobbing in their wake, are often surprised to find their careers derailed or sidelined. Nothing separates such leaders from their illusions as quickly and sharply as a crisis, because it's then they realize they haven't built the skills necessary to lead effectively during such traumatic events.

An organization's senior leadership is key before, during, and after a crisis, and its quality can determine the length, severity, and ultimate consequences of the crisis. Leaders set the tone by their example and conduct during the crisis situation. By paying attention to the components of influence (especially communication, clarity of vision and values, and caring), leaders can have a significant positive impact on the very human, emotionally charged climate that accompanies a crisis. That in turn can reduce the negative impact and duration of a crisis for the benefit of the organization.

Effective leaders often have a well-developed ability to influence others and can avoid using authoritarian or fear tactics to get results. This is an especially important capability in a crisis situation when strong leadership is essential and getting results through others using threats, pressure, and coercion is generally unproductive and can even be harmful. Influencing techniques that are effective during normal times become even more critical during a crisis. Because influencing skills are applicable during normal business situations as well as in a crisis, leaders can develop these skills before the heat of a crisis is upon them. To get the most from their developmental efforts, leaders should concentrate on the three influencing skills most critical for crisis leadership: communication, clarity of vision and values, and caring for others.

Attention to these areas is important because the idea that crisis will forge a leader, that he or she will rise to the occasion and display a depth of skill that was previously unseen, is a uniquely romantic Western notion. Such an appealing spontaneous development is rare. If your day-to-day leadership doesn't bolster trust, garner respect, inspire confidence, and connect emotionally with your direct reports, it's highly improbable that your leadership will dramatically change just because a crisis is at hand. If you don't communicate or share information, don't emphasize your personal or the organization's vision and values, and don't build strong working relationships, it is unrealistic to think that these essential crisis leadership behaviors will improve or rise to the surface in a crisis. On the other hand, if you are routinely involved with your direct reports, concerned and interested in their well-being and development, are consistent in your behavior, and display integrity,

---

 Leading with a Lighter Touch

United States Army leader experiences support the notion that heavy-handed leadership tactics like intimidation or bullying don't work in an emotionally charged crisis situation, especially in the extremely volatile combat environment. During the Vietnam War in particular, leaders who used such tactics encountered passive-aggressive behavior, insubordination, and mutiny from the soldiers serving under them. Army research revealed that a leader's use of positive influencing tactics was effective in achieving goals—even in combat. Traditional authoritarian leadership methods were found to be generally counterproductive and, in fact, alienated soldiers to the point that many times those methods produced the opposite result of what was desired.

This finding, backed by careful research, was key to transforming the army's leadership philosophy during the post–Vietnam War era. In a combat (or crisis) situation, full cooperation is necessary from every soldier, not only to accomplish the mission but also to ensure the survival of the people in the unit. As a result of its research, the army began to train its leaders in the use of positive influencing tactics that didn't rely on rank, position, or regulation. It replaced negative influencing methods like threats, coercion, punishment, humiliation, verbal abuse, and shame tactics. Army leaders who reverted to traditional heavy-handed tactics gained the reputation as being second-rate leaders and jeopardized their future opportunities to serve in troop-leading positions.

---

competence, and commitment, then you are more likely to conduct yourself in the same manner during a crisis.

Communication plays a part in crisis leadership. During a crisis people are often fearful about what has happened, what will happen, and how the crisis will affect them. It's an inescapable facet of the human element of a crisis. Information, particularly from someone in a leadership position, goes a long way in reducing fear and providing reassurance. Information can help people in an organization undergoing crisis restore their emotional balance, sense of security, and confidence.

A leader can foster and encourage an emotional connection with direct reports, communicating through word, deed, and attitude that the strong emotions employees feel during a crisis are understandable, normal, and respected. In other words, leaders should assure people in the organization that it's all right to feel emotionally stretched in these circumstances. Communicating that message helps to create a safe harbor for people to express their feelings, which is crucial in reducing the emotional impact of a crisis, promoting emotional healing, and reducing the long-term negative effects of a crisis. Without the leader's support for full communication, the crisis can have a significant negative impact on morale, attitudes, productivity, retention, and other critical organizational functions.

Clarity of vision and values plays a part in crisis leadership. Generally, both the vision and the values of the organization are created by senior leadership and are clarified, made practical, and implemented by the leaders throughout all organizational levels. A viable vision describes the direction in which the organization moves and what it will look like when it gets there. Values establish what is important to the organization. They deal with items like quality, customer service, and taking care of the employees.

A focus on organizational and individual vision and values strengthens crisis leadership by extending the influence of leaders all across the organization. A crisis has the tendency to distract people from the job that has to be done, even if it's critical to the survival of the organization. That kind of turmoil is part of the human element in a crisis. Clarity of vision, mission, objectives, and standards of conduct that are well established prior to the crisis can be foundational in holding the organization together during the crisis by providing security to its people.

Clearly established and well-understood organizational values are equally important in providing security to people in an organization during a crisis. Values tend to give the organization's employees a sense of continuity, purpose, and stability in a climate of chaos, confusion, and change. But they retain their relevancy only if the organization's leadership consistently follow and emphasize them. Organizations with strong values will in all probability handle crisis situations more effectively than those that don't. Their values hold everything together when things seem to be falling apart around them.

Caring plays a part in crisis leadership. Leadership doesn't happen in a vacuum. It requires both a leader and followers, and therefore implies a relationship between them. Because a relationship lies at the heart of leadership, and because crisis situations are fraught with emotion, leaders who are highly skilled at relating to others have a significant advantage during a crisis when it comes to influencing others to get results. Leaders who ignore the social or human element of leadership—the relationship—are not leading but only managing.

Emotions generally run high during a crisis because it usually threatens basic human needs that may be physiological or social in nature and that can affect people's sense of security and self-esteem. If people in a crisis perceive that their basic needs will not be met, they may feel such emotions as fear, anxiety, confusion, anger, and grief. These emotions inevitably result in behaviors aimed at ensuring that their needs *will* be met. In a crisis such behaviors may further aggravate the situation.

For example, there is a basic human need to feel valued and appreciated. A leader who tells direct reports that the group can't do without them and that the task before it can't be accomplished without their help is making an appeal most people can't refuse, particularly in a difficult situation. (This technique, although effective and powerful, can also have negative effects because some people may see it as manipulative. If you make such an appeal, be sure of your audience and of your motives.)

An organization's culture often reflects the attitude of its leaders, and employees throughout the organization will often emulate the behavior and attitude they see in their leaders. In making communication, clarity of vision and values, and caring part of their leadership portfolio, managers throughout the organization can play a role in handling the human side of a crisis.

What People Need

The importance of human needs and their relationship to human emotions is critical to crisis leadership. Psychologists and sociologists have spent years developing theories to explain why human beings feel, think, and behave as they do when they perceive their needs as unmet, like during a crisis. But what are these needs? When it comes to crisis leadership and the importance of influence for achieving results during difficult times, the group of needs most relevant might be defined as *social* needs. Some of these include attention, participation, acceptance, nurturing, unconditional love, and the opportunity to grow and achieve. These social needs can be of great importance to people in a crisis situation. Leaders can, through positive and supportive methods, ensure these needs are fully satisfied.

The kind of leadership that fills that role can be developed, and it can be used in any situation—including a crisis. It's the kind of leadership that positively influences others to achieve objectives. It's the kind of leadership that extends beyond a leader's direct reports to touch people outside of the leader's circle of authority, connecting with bosses, peers, and workers throughout the organization. It touches external constituents like customers, clients, suppliers, the media, and competitors. And it also reduces the severity of the impact a crisis can have on the organization and its people. It helps things return to normal as soon as possible and lessens the probability of the crisis reoccurring. Developing and then using these three key tactics of positive influence before, during, and after a crisis is key to crisis leadership.

3
PREPARING FOR CRISIS

Communication, clear vision and values, and the fostering of effective, caring relationships all directly affect how people in an organization will emotionally respond to a crisis. These three capabilities strengthen a leader's ability to help the organization and its people to weather a crisis. But more must be done. Effective leaders prepare their organizations for crisis.

Traditionally, books and articles about crisis management place a great deal of emphasis on management actions to be taken in preparation for a crisis. This focus on management functions implies that you can prepare for a crisis by writing a plan and then executing it when the crisis occurs. Certainly an effective leader is competent in such functions as planning, organizing, staffing, budgeting, controlling, and directing. But a narrow emphasis on management strategy and planning ignores the leadership necessary for putting the plan into action. That kind of approach sidesteps the human element that plays such a large role during a crisis—the needs, emotions, and behaviors of people at all levels of the organization.

Crises do not happen in isolation. Leaders may (or may not) find some comfort in knowing that in virtually every instance of a crisis, someone or some group in the organization saw it coming. Take, for example, the space shuttle *Challenger* disaster in January 1986. A checkered manufacturing and design history, documented in the *Report of the Presidential Commission on the Space Shuttle* Challenger *Accident*, revealed that several engineers at NASA and at Morton Thiokol, the contractor responsible for designing and building the space shuttle's solid rocket booster, reported what they called unacceptable flaws in the design and placement of the O-rings between the booster's joints. Even as far back as 1978, some NASA engineers warned that the O-ring design was faulty based on laboratory firing tests. Further, tests at extreme temperatures showed that the O-rings could leak. Both of these factors contributed to the explosion that destroyed the *Challenger* and killed all seven astronauts on board, setting a crisis in motion that delayed the United States space program's scientific progress several years.

The *Challenger* story is a dramatic example, but it's not unique. Often employees may have no reporting avenue, will not be listened to if they do report what they observe, or feel disconnected from the organization and therefore simply stand by and let the crisis unfold. This type of passive-aggressive, negative behavior reflects on the leadership of the organization. If the organization's leadership communicates clearly, builds relationships and connects emotionally, and highlights personal and organizational vision and values, then it is less likely that this kind of behavior will occur. These points are critical to preparing for a crisis.

Communication as Crisis Preparation

The possibility of a crisis occurring within an organization and what its plans are to deal with it must be constantly communicated to the workforce. If this is done, the response to any crisis will be less emotionally charged. Not knowing what to do is the cause of great anxiety and confusion, which leaders can reduce by communicating (even if only in a general way) what will be done in the case of various crisis situations.

Face-to-face contact remains the most effective means of communication because it promotes the emotional connection that is so crucial when a crisis does occur. Although it may be time consuming and extremely difficult with the geographic dispersion common to today's organizations, an effective communication strategy might involve leaders meeting with small groups in their own work areas to encourage an informal conversation. This approach is very effective because it allows for questions and comments that might never be asked or shared in a larger group. It also allows leaders and managers to ask questions and get responses they might not get from a larger group. The setting of an informal conversation can also help meet a key emotional need of people to belong to the larger group, which is a source of strength leaders can tap into when a crisis occurs.

Leaders should direct their communication toward all levels of the organization—not just to the highest or lowest echelons. Also, remember that sharing information isn't a one-time event but should be a regular practice. When a crisis does occur, leaders don't want their communicating to seem odd because they never bothered to do it before. As they communicate, leaders at all levels of the organization should follow a rule of three Rs: review, repeat, and reinforce.

 World War II British General and Corps Commander Sir Brian Horrocks often took a large map outlining the current tactical situation and traveled up and down his front lines, stopping to personally speak with his soldiers. Unannounced, he would stop and personally brief his soldiers, even if there were only five or six of them present. He felt this form of personal communication was necessary in preparing for a crisis (in this case, combat) because it allowed him to emotionally connect with his soldiers, reinforce the vision of what they were fighting for, and show the soldiers their senior leaders cared about them and understood the situation.

During this stage of crisis preparation, a goal leaders might consider for their communications efforts is establishing and promoting common understanding. The basis of this understanding is to create a consistency across the organization at all levels as to the clarity and usefulness of procedures and directives that the organization will bear when a crisis develops. Often a leader will find that instructions are not satisfactorily followed because they have not been communicated clearly and logically. It helps to clearly outline the personal advantages that direct reports will gain by following the organization's directives and the instructions that come from their leaders. (Think of this tactic as an answer to the "What's in it for me?" question.) Any persuasive argument should pass the "common-sense test"—are the actions that leaders are directing practical, balanced, and appropriate for the situation?

To accomplish this communications task, use common words and short sentences, have direct reports restate directions after receiving them (have them put directives into their own words), and review key ideas. These tactics are especially helpful before a crisis hits because when that happens, emotions run high and listening skills are reduced.

Without a real and obvious advantage, direct reports may feel less ownership of the challenges brought on by the crisis and may not support the organization's solutions. Their efforts may be halfhearted and carried out because of a sense of compliance rather than of commitment. In a crisis, leaders don't want to be met with questions and hesitations over basic actions designed to ensure the organization's survival.

Planning with Vision and Values

If there is a clarity of vision and values throughout the organization, then leaders can use it to focus their crisis planning. That vision and the organization's values can help define the actions needed to detect an impending crisis and serve as a hub to ensure all efforts designed to deal with the crisis are consistent and in line with the mission, goals, and objectives of the organization. They also provide an element of stability and security for the employees that can significantly reduce the degree of anxiety they feel when a crisis hits.

As part of both crisis preparation and establishing organizational values, an organization's leaders should direct the establishment of standard operating procedures designed to prevent and/or detect an impending crisis. (A detailed explanation and sample worksheet related to these procedures can be found in Appendix A, "The Crisis Action Plan (CAP)," on pages 75–80.) These procedures have several specific purposes. They describe the signals or indicators that might alert the organization that a crisis is imminent and what actions should be taken at that time. These actions can include detailed rules that, if followed by employees, can avert a crisis situation altogether. These procedures also assess the organization's key vulnerabilities regarding a crisis. Other rules or standards might include an inspection or audit system that ensures employees are following the prescribed procedures and other established operational rules and regulations. Overall, and perhaps most importantly, the organization's standard operating procedures should reflect and support its vision and values.

As you examine your crisis leadership preparedness, think of the qualities that make a good teacher. You most likely had at least

---

 Five times I was a unit commander in the army, and each time I constantly communicated the need to prepare for the ultimate mission—combat. Every presentation, class, or short discourse I gave focused on what we were doing or should be doing in getting ready for when we would have to deploy for combat. This was not a popular discussion for some of my soldiers who, understandably, did not want to go into combat. But the possibility of combat, as with any crisis, doesn't go away because it's ignored. The more attention leaders pay to the possibility, the better prepared their people and their organizations are when crisis does occur.

---

one teacher before or during your career whose approach, style, and character enhanced his or her effect on you. In many ways, to be an effective leader is to be an effective teacher. The leader's teaching skills are particularly significant prior to a crisis. They help explain the organization's vision, mission, and values, and the expectations associated with each. Teaching implies that some individual attention is given to the learner. The more attention leaders can give to those with whom they are sharing the organization's vision, mission, and values, the more focus these key items will receive during a crisis. If the leader does a good job of teaching these things, they can serve as a source of stability in a time of confusion. Without a good teacher to spread the word and reinforce the lessons of visions and values, an organization's people might as well act as if that vision and those values don't exist. When a crisis strikes, that's not the perspective you want your employees to have.

Caring and Connecting as Preparation for Crisis

A clear vision based on clear values can yield a plan that leaders can communicate throughout the organization. But how can a leader prepare people to adopt and follow the plan? It takes more than a good plan and open communication. The most effective way is for the leader to practice behaviors that validate, affirm, and recognize the organization's employees. Experience demonstrates that certain behaviors are extremely effective in building interpersonal relationships in the organization between leaders and their direct reports. These relationships are extremely important in creating a climate in which employees are responsive to a leader's efforts to deal with their emotional needs once a crisis occurs. These so-called caring actions must be sincere and authentic. If they aren't, the employees will pick up on it immediately and the result will be the reverse of what was intended. If leaders can't be genuine in implementing caring behaviors, then they should avoid them. And they had better hope that a crisis never occurs.

Two especially effective caring behaviors that can have a tremendous influence on how people will respond if and when a crisis occurs are feedback and coaching. CCL research has determined that giving feedback is a skill, employees want it in order to know where they stand, and leaders are generally hesitant in giving it. If as a leader you give feedback and you do it well, that interaction can form an emotional connection that during an actual crisis will reap great benefits in employee loyalty, support, patience, and cooperation.

CCL recommends a method of feedback called Situation–Behavior–Impact (SBI). CCL has found SBI to be extremely effective for two reasons. One, it reduces the defensiveness of the recipient since it focuses on the impact of the behavior and does not judge the person or seek motives. Two, this method makes it easier and more comfortable to deliver feedback because it focuses on the impact of a person's behavior and not the person's personality.

The first stage of the SBI method asks the person giving the feedback (in this case the leader who is preparing for crisis by further developing effective relationships) to describe the situation in which the behavior occurred. At the next stage, the leader describes the behavior during that particular situation. Behavior shouldn't be interpreted as to its motives, but rather limited to observable actions, verbal comments, nonverbal behaviors and signals (body language), and mannerisms (which can be a combination of several kinds of behaviors). In the third stage of SBI, the leader describes the impact of the behavior within that situation. For example, the leader might address the consequences of the behavior, the impact it has on others, and whether or not the behavior was effective or ineffective in that particular situation.

The feedback process works best when the relationship between the feedback giver and receiver is based on mutual trust, respect, and dignity. The person receiving the feedback should understand that the leader giving the feedback is doing so for developmental purposes. A leader giving feedback can't assume the person receiving the feedback is aware of his or her behavior, as described during the feedback process, or its impact, either positive or negative. Each person responds differently to feedback and leaders should expect surprises. Some people are more extroverted than others and will immediately respond with what they intend to do to address the feedback. More introverted people might need a day or so to process what they have heard and to reflect on the feedback.

To make the feedback process more effective in establishing and maintaining a caring, effective relationship that can withstand and respond to the rigors of a crisis, leaders can keep some of these tips and best practices in mind:

- strive to create an organizational culture that supports a safe and positive feedback environment;
- feedback should be ongoing, not just once a year during a performance appraisal;
- give feedback promptly—when opportunities arise and the observations and information are fresh;
- be observant and sensitive to what is going on around you, especially regarding people in the organization;
- make your feedback as specific and simple as possible;
- feedback should be balanced, not just negative—but don't "sandwich" negative feedback between positive feedback or it might not be heard;
- deliver feedback with some grace, in a kind, honest, and candid fashion;

- listen attentively to the receiver;
- allow the receiver to tell you what he or she will do with the feedback; provide suggestions and guidance, but don't mandate actions;
- if the feedback relates to performance problems, schedule the feedback session for a private, focused, and structured meeting;
- be aware of your personal assumptions and biases—your feedback says as much about you as it does about the receiver.

There are other points to consider regarding the use of feedback. In preparing for a crisis, it's most necessary not just to memorize definitive guidelines about delivering feedback, but rather to understand how to use feedback to establish a caring relationship that will guarantee employee loyalty, tolerance, collaboration, and teamwork in a crisis situation.

In addition to feedback, coaching can be a significant action for developing effective relationships in preparation for a crisis. CCL has developed a highly usable approach to coaching that each leader can adjust to his or her own style and unique situation. This kind of coaching is drawn from years of CCL experience in leadership development initiatives and relies on the lessons people draw from their own experiences of facing challenges. CCL calls the method Assessment–Challenge–Support (ACS). This coaching method provides an excellent framework for leaders to use in developmental activities with their direct reports and other employees. It also confirms to employees that the organization's leadership cares about their individual development.

The ACS method involves assessing a person's strengths and weaknesses related to a given performance area. The next step after that is defining a challenge, such as a job assignment, that will stretch the person being coached. That creates an opportunity for the person to develop skills in areas where weaknesses exist and learn more efficient ways to use available strengths. The leader and the organization can provide different means of support (such as mentoring or training). Through this process the organization and the individual leaders involved in the coaching can bolster employee allegiance, dependability, and trust when a crisis erupts.

Although this brief discussion isn't meant to replace a fuller explanation of coaching practices, a coaching session using the ACS method might include many of the following steps:

- the leader makes opening remarks with the goal of creating a safe environment;
- the leader clarifies the purpose of the session and the topic(s) to be discussed;
- the leader works to make sure that the bulk of the conversation is coming from the person being coached, not the coach;
- the leader, as coach, facilitates the coaching session by asking open-ended questions such as these: What do you think about . . . ? Can you tell me more about . . . ? What do you mean by . . . ?;
- the leader-coach clarifies comments the person being coached makes by periodically paraphrasing what has been said and, near the end of the session, by summarizing what was said;
- during the session, the leader-coach pays attention to the body language, facial expressions, eye contact, tone of voice, choice of words, and other behavioral signals of the person being coached;
- the person being coached sets goals at the end of the session with the help of the leader-coach;

- the leader-coach helps establish how the goals will be achieved and measured;
- the leader-coach offers support such as resources, time, experience, and so on;
- when the session is brought to closure, the date and time of the next session (if appropriate and needed) is established by both sides.

Feedback and coaching are powerful tools for the fostering of caring and effective relationships and for developing people so they are ready to act when a crisis occurs. But there are other practices a leader can engage to foster those relationships. Simple yet effective actions a leader can take to demonstrate caring and genuine concern for the emotional well-being of direct reports include, but aren't limited to, the following:

- greet people by name;
- maintain and display a positive, optimistic, upbeat attitude;
- smile at and shake hands with employees;
- say "thank you" for a job well done and use specific examples when complimenting individuals on performance;
- follow through on promises;
- be patient;
- listen attentively;
- be courteous to all and avoid coarse language;
- remain emotionally steady, balanced, moderate, and levelheaded;
- solicit input from employees on events and actions that impact them;

- keep employees informed about events and actions that affect them;
- avoid gossip, passing rumors, or bashing one's peers, boss, or the organization;
- use appropriate and well-timed stories and humor;
- ask appropriate and sincere questions about individual employee interests (family, hobbies, and activities, for example);
- be present, visible, and available;
- encourage efforts and risk taking;
- treat others humanely and with dignity and respect;
- look for ways to further develop and build up employees' self-esteem and self-worth;
- appreciate and respect diversity;
- praise and compliment often and as soon as possible after an employee's positive action;
- don't delay counseling or disciplining employees when it's called for;
- use dignity when disciplining employees—don't resort to humiliation or personal destruction;
- answer emotionally charged questions and comments with calm and quiet;
- avoid arrogance, conceit, and unseemly pride;
- promptly return employee phone calls and e-mails;
- set an example of integrity;
- carry yourself as a leader and someone who is to be respected;
- be clear in your expectations and explanations;
- set a good example by taking care of yourself physically, handling stress well, and leading a balanced life.

Connections, Commitment, and Confidence
From interviews with thousands of combat veterans, the United States Army's post–World War II research revealed that those military units that had high trust and confidence in their unit leaders showed a low rate of combat fatigue or shell shock. Conversely, those units whose soldiers reported that they neither trusted nor liked their leaders showed an extremely high rate of combat fatigue or shell shock, sometimes as much as ten times more than the units who trusted their leaders.

The units with low rates of combat fatigue reported several consistent themes. Their leaders clearly cared about their soldiers and would not consciously do anything self-serving or operationally impractical that might needlessly get someone injured or killed. They treated soldiers with respect and dignity. Their leaders were honest and comfortable to talk to—they came across as authentic and could be counted on to keep their word. They were professionally competent and always had some idea of what to do that made sense in regard to the unit's situation. They were effective communicators and ensured that the soldiers under their leadership always knew what was going on and what could be expected.

Those leaders whose units had large numbers of battle fatigue incidents displayed few of those positive leadership actions. Instead, they kept their soldiers in the dark, took casualties that the unit's personnel thought were unnecessary, and just didn't seem to care about the soldiers or value them as human beings. They used their rank and position to get privileges that they did not share with the troops. They also did not share the same hardships that their troops did. There was no emotional connection between the leaders and their soldiers, and as a result there was a dramatic loss of confidence in their leadership.

Preparing for any situation, including a crisis, makes it necessary to assess strengths and weaknesses, to pinpoint skills, and to acknowledge performance gaps. As a leader preparing yourself and your organization for handling a crisis, you may learn from feedback and other sources that you are not particularly noted for caring. You may see upon reflection that you don't possess a clear personal vision based on your own authentic and meaningful values or that you can't articulate the organization's values and vision. You may come to understand that you don't emphasize communication in your style of leadership. If any of these indications ring true for you, take it as a signal to become more caring, communicate more effectively, and cast a clearer vision and value system.

Don't wait until a crisis strikes to find out your leadership skills are wanting in these areas. The skills you bring to the table in normal operations are the same you will depend on in a crisis, only they will be amplified in their effect. In preparing for a crisis, leaders can regularly work to improve the skills, traits, and perspectives that will make them more effective in a crisis situation.

4
LEADING DURING CRISIS

The time for planning is over. The crisis is upon you and can be felt throughout the organization. It doesn't matter whether or not you have developed a crisis action plan (as described in Appendix A, pages 75–80). A crisis sets its own timetable. It doesn't wait for you to draw up a plan or to develop leadership skills. But if your organization has developed a strategy for dealing with a crisis, and you focus much of your leadership efforts on the human elements (having assessed and developed your communication and relationship skills, developed a clarity of vision that's aligned with your personal values and the values of your organization, and worked to foster and maintain effective relationships), then you have the opportunity to successfully lead your people through a volatile situation.

There are several specific things leaders can do immediately upon being notified that a crisis is imminent. These actions help reduce anxieties and fears that arise from a perceived threat to meeting human needs. First, there must be a concerted focus on fact finding. Initial reports are generally inaccurate because the people relaying the information tend to overstate or understate the direness of the situation or because the reports are too full of emotion to be of any real value. One of your first actions should be to send a trusted agent to the scene of the crisis with the sole purpose of gathering information and reporting back to you and your staff. If the crisis is serious enough, the organization's senior leader should go to the crisis area. Further, if it is a level 3 crisis (there is loss of life, significant property damage, or a perceived threat to the survival of the company), a number of actions should be taken simultaneously. Leaders shouldn't assume that these actions are too simple or have no application to their organization. Consider how your company would respond to any of those crises described on pages 4–5. Are you ready to lead in such circumstances? Is your organization prepared to act? Do your direct reports understand the plan, and are they willing to implement it?

Leaders who understand the connection between emotion and behavior will be more effective during a crisis because they will understand how to meet the needs of people in the organization and so influence their behavior. That connection describes a sequence that starts with the crisis, results in an emotion in answer to a threatened need, and is followed by a move to action and subsequent behavior. Leaders who are conscious of this sequence can respond to it so the behaviors of those impacted by the crisis are positive, balanced, and desirable. It's important to remember that emotions and feelings are not by themselves negative or bad. They are powerful internal signals that tell people what they should pay attention to, and they play a major role in our overall health and well-being. If uncontrolled, however, emotions can sometimes lead to socially unacceptable behaviors. Leaders need to take emotions into consideration—their own and others'—because the people in their organizations, on their teams, and in their larger community behave in ways consistent with their emotions. In a crisis emotions can become unbalanced and lead to behaviors that may be uncharacteristic. A key to crisis leadership is anticipating this chain of events and leading in such a way as to return balance to others in the organization.

To leverage the power of their understanding about the connection between emotions and behavior, leaders can once again turn their eyes to the three critical components of crisis leadership. They can focus on communicating, establishing clarity about personal and organizational vision and values, and displaying their care for people at all levels of the organization. Leadership aimed at meeting

In the early 1990s John Mayer and Peter Salovey introduced a concept that has since become known as *emotional intelligence*, or *EQ*. This kind of intelligence describes a person's ability to understand his or her own emotions as well as the emotions of others, and it describes a person's ability to act and behave according to that understanding. In several books that popularized emotional intelligence, Daniel Goleman listed *social awareness* and *social skills* as two of the five competency areas of EQ. Social awareness includes empathy, political savvy, appreciating diverse perspectives, and being sensitive to other people's feelings. It's essentially the ability to detect and be responsive to the emotions, moods, intentions, needs, and desires of others. Social skills include being discerning about what is going on around you, communicating well-timed comments and observations, possessing a general competence level at a variety of social settings, and positively managing emotions in others.

CCL research has found that one cause of derailment involves deficits in interpersonal relationships, or what might be described as emotional intelligence. Alternatively, effective leaders are similar in that they all possess a high degree of EQ.

essential human needs—social, security, and acceptance—can inspire positive or, at worst, neutral behaviors from your direct reports. Small actions such as being available, listening, sharing available information, commending those who do outstanding work during the crisis, remaining positive and upbeat, and giving people time off to take care of personal issues related to the crisis sound so simple, but they aren't always easy to carry out. Many issues and external agencies (such as the news media and stockholders) will demand your time and attention. Like anyone else in the organization, you are likely to face an emotional and physical drain. But acting to promote an emotional connection, regardless of how you feel, is an essential piece of crisis leadership.

Communicating During the Crisis

Communicating clearly and often during a crisis is essential, but can be difficult. A leader has some advantage if the organization's crisis action plan (CAP) has set up some communication guidelines. With or without a guide, however, the bottom line is simple: keep internal and external communication lines open and working so that everyone is informed and they don't have to make up their own stories about the crisis.

Who to talk to. Based on the seriousness of the crisis (that is, the perceived level of the crisis), the organization's senior leaders must also decide who should be informed, when, and how. These stakeholders might include the organization's employees, community groups, local government leaders and officials, government regulators, stockholders, customers, suppliers, the local neighborhood, and the news media.

From the outset of the crisis, senior leaders should be out among the employees sharing what they know has occurred, explaining what is being done about it now (and what steps are being taken so it won't happen again), and, when possible, describing implications for the future. Leaving employees out of the information loop during a crisis can be a major mistake. An organization's employees are a loud voice for the organization. They will undoubtedly tell their immediate circle of influence what they think happened, based on what they know. Their knowledge can be the truth that they heard from their leaders or it can be the rumors and gossip they heard in the hallway. If they are not told what is going on, their fears and anxieties about the crisis can turn into anger, distrust, and even revenge. And the organization will become the target of these emotions and possibly of destructive behavior.

What the organization's leadership initially communicates to the organization's internal and external stakeholders should include (and generally be limited to) the known details of the situation, what went wrong and why, what is being done to deal with the immediate situation, and the actions that are and will be taken to ensure the situation does not happen again. Leaders should stick to the facts and avoid conjecture. In the early stages of the crisis it is also wise to avoid speculating about future implications of the crisis. If pressed, leaders can say that the greater implications are unknown at the present time but will be analyzed. Under no circumstances should leaders fabricate or change information with the intent to deceive. It's certain that such actions will be found out and actually exacerbate the crisis.

There are immediate and specific communication actions that leaders can take to reduce the negative impact of the crisis and also sustain (and perhaps even improve) relationships with stakeholders. Some of the most important external stakeholders during a crisis are the media, and clear, consistent communications with them is critical during a crisis. The news media can extend the leader's communication resources. If handled correctly, a leader can use the media to exert a powerful, positive, emotional impact on all

A Gulf War experience confirmed to me that it is essential to not only distribute the information that is known but to also monitor what your people are telling others. At one point in our deployment I called my wife to give her an update of our activities for the battalion's family support group. She told me she had heard that two of my battalion's soldiers had died from drinking poisoned water. This wasn't true, but is a good example of how information can get corrupted as it moves from one part of an organization to another.

What really happened was this: On a routine check of our water sources, soldiers took a reading that showed the source contained some contamination. Further checks indicated that this was a false reading. However, as different soldiers called home (the army provided a range of communication options to its soldiers), the story became embellished to the point that one soldier told his family in North Carolina that two soldiers were dead as a result of the water contamination. This experience reinforces the need for the leader to communicate complete, timely, and accurate information during a crisis, and to monitor the veracity of that information as it moves through the organization or outside to the public.

stakeholders, and in particular on the organization's employees. For example, leaders in an organization can use the media to achieve such positive goals as

- gathering and distributing vital information
- promoting understanding of the situation
- squelching rumors
- acting as an early warning system
- activating emergency response units
- furnishing current and specific traffic activity information (for example, detours and business, activity, or school closings)
- giving evacuation information and alerting the public to possible danger

To achieve these and other goals, there are specific actions that leaders can take to ensure that they are communicating what they want and need to say to the media. Many of these actions, some of which are described below, were learned the hard way. Companies that didn't use these tactics suffered damaged reputations or worse.

Write a formal press release and distribute it to the media as soon as possible after the event. A rapid response helps the organization contain the story, reduces the flow of false or negative information, creates positive perceptions, and reduces misconceptions. Most importantly, information helps reduce the fears and emotions of employees and other stakeholders who are directly affected by the crisis. By going on the offensive, the organization regains some control over events. Leaders should act as the prime information sources and shouldn't shy away from admitting that they don't know all of the facts if that is the case. If they don't tell a full story the media will look to other sources for information—including employees who don't know all the facts but are more than happy to share "what they have heard," or, even worse, a disgruntled employee who might deliver negative, damaging, or even false information.

Take the initiative. Meet with media representatives. Distribute your message through every channel possible to ensure that all stakeholders receive it. Make all statements simple and clear, and leave no room for interpretation. Media statements should address, to varying degrees, the who, what, when, where, how, and why of the crisis. (This tactic is helpful in clarifying the situation, not just for the media, but also for the employees and even the organization's leaders.) It is totally acceptable for a leader to say, "I don't have all the information now, but this is what I do know. More information will be given as it becomes available."

Be truthful, accurate, and honest. This strategy may have unintended or unexpected consequences, but the consequences of misleading stakeholders or especially the media will certainly be negative and damaging. Leaders who try to protect their organizations or themselves with a cover-up or by stonewalling will damage the credibility of both. Credibility and trust are easily lost in a crisis without lying—why guarantee their loss by not telling the truth? The leader's openness and honesty are essential ingredients for the company's long-term reputation and for its survival in a crisis. When leaders tell the truth they don't have to remember what they said at previous meetings.

Apologize if necessary. People are more forgiving of leaders who admit mistakes and promise to correct them than they are of leaders who have neither the character nor courage to admit wrong. If injuries or deaths resulted from the crisis, emphasize concern for victims and their families. Obviously, this kind of situation calls for a compassionate, sympathetic, and sensitive demeanor and tone. If carried out empathetically and sincerely, an apology can ease the emotions and concerns of listeners. This is crisis leadership at its best.

Explain fully and clearly. It's essential during a crisis for the leader to explain what went wrong, why it went wrong, what is being done about it, and what is being done to ensure it will not happen again. Avoid technical details or overly complicated statistics because reciting them does nothing to reduce the emotional impact of the crisis and can actually stir up negative emotions. The media may view this type of information as "corporate speak" or double-talk, designed to shift the focus away from the cause of the crisis. Make your messages consistent and your explanations credible. Anything less opens the leader and the organization up to all sorts of questions, misinterpretations, and conjecture. If you have made it a practice of explaining organizational strategy, tactics, vision, and values during normal times, then you will be prepared to make these explanations during a crisis—and your audience is more likely to trust your explanations.

Evaluate what you communicate. There is a delicate balance between sharing too much information and not sharing enough. The responsibility for finding that balance falls to the organization's leaders. The information they share with the public through the media and the manner in which they share it has a tremendous effect on how the crisis is perceived. Judge the information for its potential to have a negative impact. Leaders can't assume the public will view the crisis as they do, and that difference can mitigate or aggravate the crisis.

Monitor the media. What the media is reporting should be carefully scrutinized. If the information is not accurate or doesn't tell the whole story, it should be challenged with the intent of setting the record straight with the truth. The relationship between the media and an organization during a crisis isn't necessarily adversarial, and it doesn't do anything to alleviate the crisis if you alienate them, treat them as a nuisance, or inhibit their efforts. On the other hand, providing honest and clear information through the media channels can have a positive emotional impact on your employees and the public, which can benefit your organization during a crisis and display effective and positive leadership.

How to tell your message. In facing anxious employees and families, and an interested public, leaders should keep a calm, confident, and controlled demeanor. A crisis often causes so much tension and anxiety that the people in the organization may not listen as well as they might in ordinary circumstances. Repeat key points and themes several times so listeners, who are wrestling with some powerful emotions during the crisis, don't miss them. Often in a crisis organizational leaders give information to the news media, customers, shareholders, and the community and forget about the most important audience of all: the organization's employees. Prior to any communication effort, assess who needs the information and communicate with that perspective in mind.

Even information that isn't particularly positive is essential because it discourages rumors. The effect of inaccurate, made-up information is worse than the effect of accurate, negative information. Leaders can limit the impact of rumors by sharing with their direct reports the information that is available and also by communicating what they don't know. The communication channels available for this task include e-mail, voice mail, memos, letters to employees' homes, the organization's Web site or intranet, telephone hot lines, bulletin boards, TV and radio reports, and face-to-face meetings.

As they communicate to others, leaders should remain aware of their own feelings about the crisis and its impact on the organization, their direct reports, and themselves. Leaders can gain a great deal of credibility if they are open and honest enough to say that they are experiencing some of the same emotions. Direct reports can identify with a leader who experiences the same emotions as they do. This helps employees see their leaders as authentic, which supports the emotional connection so essential to successfully navigating a crisis.

Clarity of Vision and Values

Leadership implies being out in front and showing the way. During a crisis, leaders must live the vision and values they've defined for and communicated to the people in their organization so that others have an example of effective behavior to follow. They need to set an example, take responsibility, and be visible. Rudolph Guiliani, in his book *Leadership*, writes that two of the most important things for leaders to have is a set of beliefs and an understanding of how they developed them.

Set the example. It's not enough to have guiding values. Leaders must actively and consciously practice them as a way of setting an example for others to follow. Leadership by example, not just by word, has a tremendous emotional impact on an organization's people during a crisis. Direct reports and others in the organization will closely observe their leader to assure themselves that things are under control and going to be all right. Leaders should train themselves to project an image of calm and confidence regardless of the "hockey game" going on in their stomachs. If the leader appears to be hurried, harried, or visually shaken and distraught, the impact of the crisis can actually be amplified for employees and others.

Leaders in the organization should set the example by emphasizing and following the vision and values as expressed in the organization's standard operating procedures, mission statement, and best practices. This provides continuity for the employees, increases their sense of security, provides a common focus, and sets a direction with which the employees have a degree of comfort. A crisis is not the time to come up with new rules, regulations, processes, and procedures. Such actions only further aggravate the crisis. Leading by the examples described in its operating procedures and extolled in its vision and values highlights the kinds of behavior that become part of the organization's culture. For leaders to pay lip service to the vision and values and not personally follow them neutralizes the impact of those values and, even worse, makes them into a joke. Leaders should always remember that modeling desired behavior is an excellent way to ensure others will behave in the same manner.

Take responsibility. In a crisis, even if the leader did nothing to cause the crisis, he or she must accept responsibility to resolve the situation. If the leader was responsible for the crisis, he or she should be morally courageous enough to stand up and publicly accept that responsibility. Effective leaders don't wait for events to resolve themselves. They take charge of the situation, get the needed information, and control and manage events. Failure to do so is abdicating one's leadership responsibility.

Be visible. It is especially important in times of crisis that those in leadership positions be present, visible, and available. Visibility takes on a special importance during a crisis. It sends the message that the leader is engaged, concerned, and actively taking part in the resolution of the problem. It lets people throughout the organization see how its values and vision are enacted in times of duress. When people see their leader out in front during a crisis—particularly the top leader—they understand that everyone in the organization is in the situation together and that things will be fine. A leader who remains invisible raises questions, increases anxiety, and causes the crisis recovery period to last longer.

Caring During a Crisis

A crisis generally threatens a number of basic human needs, such as safety and security. By maintaining relationships and using them effectively during the crisis, a leader can keep tabs on how well or poorly those needs are being met for employees and others connected to the organization. When needs are not met, or are perceived as not met, emotions such as fear, confusion, anger, and grief rise up. In turn these emotions cause people to behave in a way that ensures their needs are met. Some of those behaviors can be negative and may worsen the crisis. A leader who pays attention to relationships will more likely recognize these responses, understand the primary emotional needs, and respond by meeting the needs of those being led.

Sincerity marks a leader's caring as authentic. Leadership that carries the mark of sincerity is a key element to effective relationships. People read, respect, and can relate to authenticity. It is something that cannot be made up. What direct reports or peers would not respond to a leader they can talk to, who doesn't put on airs, and who doesn't make others feel inferior? Such leaders can laugh at themselves, have a sense of humor, make mistakes, and can admit those mistakes. During a crisis people see them as going through the same things as everyone else, as having the same concerns, and as having an understanding of the situation and a plan for action.

Relationships must be built and maintained over the long term. Such relationships and the perceptions they inspire don't just happen. Effective leaders display caring, concern, and compassion time and time again. The relationships they build and maintain form an empowering and participative environment that supports an organization during a crisis. The important point to remember is that a leader's caring and concern must be authentic. If it's not sincere but manipulative, people in the organization will quickly pick up on that, and your influence as a leader will decrease. Many organizations claim that their most important resource is their people—you can read it on the posters they hang in conference rooms and hallways. If the leadership doesn't act out this sentiment, consistently and sincerely, it becomes nothing more than a hallway joke. It would be better not to even bother with such a message than to communicate that idea and have it not be the truth (or be seen as not true).

Shared experiences strengthen relationships. Strong and effective relationships derive from, among other things, positive emotional connections. Developing these strong emotional connections can actually reduce the immediate negative impact of a crisis, its short- and long-term effects on the organization, and its long-term impact on employees. But what exactly are these emotional connections? They might best be defined as a bond that develops as a result of mutual appreciation, similar perspective, and successful negotiation of a variety of shared experiences. These opportunities help leaders and their direct reports develop a sense of community, camaraderie, and bonding. When this kind of connection exists before a crisis, it makes the crisis much easier to manage. If a leader has not taken time to develop this connection, a crisis can actually be the catalyst for its development. The benefits such a connection brings to a crisis situation (and even to routine operations) include setting the foundation for effective communication; reducing fear, confusion, insecurity, and the sense of personal isolation; and bolstering confidence in a positive outcome.

During a crisis, leaders who recognize the importance of effective relationships keep watch over the organization's emotional barometer and are sensitive to the nonverbal emotional signals of people in the organization. Often a crisis can draw people closer together. It can build camaraderie and a sense of community among those who have lived through the experience. A sensitive and discerning leader can take advantage of this sense of community with activities designed to commemorate, memorialize, and remember. For example, leaders can give employees affected by the crisis paid leave. If the crisis is severe, leaders can provide immediate access to counselors and ensure that short- and long-term counseling is available. They can send letters to employee families explaining what has happened and call the organization's geographically dispersed staff, if any. Another activity, sometimes overlooked, is the provision of spiritual support opportunities, such as a memorial service, prayer meetings, a meditation room, and facilitated discussion/support groups with trained facilitators.

Solving problems and conflicts that threaten effective relationships. There are other elements to forging strong relationships that rise in importance during a crisis. One is the skill to solve problems. A crisis is certainly a problem, and the leader's ability to solve it or to be part of its solution is essential, not only in subduing the crisis but also in helping others in the organization return to an emotionally balanced place. If leaders cannot effectively solve problems or their techniques actually aggravate the existing problem, their standing and reputation will fall.

Strong Connections, Strong Rewards

During my service as an airborne battalion commander in the Gulf War in the year prior to Desert Shield, I made a concentrated effort to connect with my soldiers using the techniques described in these pages. I found these leadership methods to be very successful and validated in a number of significant ways. For example, the most severe infractions of discipline in the unit, during an entire eight-month period operating in extremely dangerous and harsh conditions, were two speeding tickets issued by the military police. After the war the unit received a Meritorious Unit Commendation from the army for the efficient manner in which it accomplished its mission. Of greatest importance and significance, however, is the fact that all 600 of the unit's soldiers who were deployed to the Persian Gulf returned to the United States alive—the signature moment of my leadership career.

Another component of the leader's relational and problem-solving skills that's crucial during a crisis is an ability to resolve conflict. The stress and pressure of a crisis inevitably causes friction and tension between employees at all levels—including those at the top of the organization. These conflicts can be very divisive and can cause animosities that might last well beyond the end of the crisis. Further, conflict can intensify and even exacerbate emotional needs among people in the organization. Leaders who develop the skill to effectively resolve conflict in normal operations will have a powerful tool when a crisis erupts. Such a situation is difficult enough to handle without the challenge of managing conflict between direct reports, peers, and bosses.

Reflection that rejuvenates relationships. With all of this focus on relationships and leading others, it's important to remember that leaders also need to reflect and keep tabs on their own emotional reactions during a crisis. They should be aware of their emotions, their reactions to stress, and how others perceive them in the organization. Leaders at all levels in the organization will want to behave in a manner that mitigates the crisis situation rather than aggravates it. For ideas and examples, refer to Appendix B on page 81.

Many things can occur during a crisis that might move a leader to react negatively. These may include difficult questions from the news media, unrealistic requests from employees, unfounded criticisms from any number of sources, or time-sensitive inquiries from outside stakeholders or regulatory agencies. Leaders who can articulate and who practice their own values are able to let negative comments roll off their backs. For example, under the stress and pressure of the crisis some employees may say negative things that they would not normally say. An effective way for leaders to deal with these comments during a crisis is to understand them as a result of stress, to ignore them and not hold people responsible for them. Those guilty of saying things they shouldn't have said will later appreciate this response and hold the leader in higher regard for it. That kind of self-control from the leader's position helps to sustain credibility and ensure that the emotional needs of those being led are met.

Another aspect of reflection is spiritual sensitivity, in whatever individual or collective sense it is practiced. During stressful situations, it provides support out of a notion that there is a higher power that can be relied on to assist and control those things that humans cannot. When leaders make it possible for people in an organization to connect to a higher power and ask for help, share concerns, and express gratitude, those activities can reduce stress, provide internal peace, and calm emotions.

Stay tough and resilient. Credibility is a valuable leadership commodity during a crisis. It's built on consistency, but consistency isn't just the ability to do the same thing over and over. It's also the ability to spring back from negative comments and to adapt to rapid changes, to be resilient. Mary Lynn Pulley and Michael

Wakefield write in *Building Resiliency: How to Thrive in Times of Change* that resiliency is important because change is so pervasive. It's hard to imagine change as dramatic as that brought about by chaos, and resiliency creates a continuity of effective leadership around which people in an organization can rally. Leadership consistency is like the smooth ride of a well-engineered car—the car's suspension system adapts to the bumps in the road to protect the passengers and to provide stability. In the same way, a leader who can handle change and difficulty with flexibility, courage, and optimism protects others in the organization, provides stability in a tumultuous environment, and inspires trust.

Resiliency is a reflection of the mental toughness required to keep your leadership on the road and moving forward during the twists and turns of a crisis. During a crisis, leaders at all levels are faced with all kinds of extremely unpleasant possibilities, such as serious injury to themselves or others, the destruction of property and equipment, or worse. They must be resilient and mentally tough enough to handle the situation. There can be no indifference or resignation. When the leader hangs tough, it shows others in the organization that someone cares enough about them and their welfare to take the punishment and to keep springing back. To quit or resign is not an option because it would result in the loss of all influence and credibility.

 Mental toughness is a key part of leadership training in the military. In a combat situation it's possible that a leader could lose a number of soldiers. Sometimes only the leader's mental toughness allows the survivors to carry on after enemy contact and provides the necessary leadership for guiding the group. This is an extreme example, but the principle for leaders in nonmilitary organizations is the same. People in your organization will look to their leaders for consistent behavior that reflects personal vision and values, adheres to the organization's mission, and remains consistent in its pursuit of a solution to the crisis.

Communicating, emphasizing the organization's vision and values, keeping tabs on the emotional pulse of the organization's people, paying attention to relationships, and using a measure of self-awareness and self-control all maintain a leader's credibility and serve to meet the needs of people undergoing a crisis. These actions demonstrate an investment in your direct reports, your organization, and yourself. They are time-proven ways of gaining the support of others by supporting them in their own efforts. Consistent leadership along these lines builds an emotional connection that helps everyone support the organization, and it pays big dividends in a crisis because the people in the organization are more likely to pull together to resolve the situation when they follow a sincere and authentic example set by their leaders. The only other path is to dissolve into individual turmoil.

5
LEADERSHIP AFTER THE CRISIS

A crisis may end, but it doesn't just fade away. Leaders can take a number of important and influential actions to ensure their organization and its employees not only recover but also prepare for a future crisis. But how does a leader recognize the end of the present crisis? Among others, indications that the crisis has passed might include such facts as

- the news media is no longer covering the story or making it a priority;
- the organization has returned to its routine operations, or business as usual;
- inquiries about the crisis from external groups or agencies such as the government, community, customers, suppliers, employee families, shareholders, or other stakeholders have dropped considerably;
- rumors and employee anxiety have returned to normal levels.

Rebuild and Reassure

Two important goals of leadership following a crisis are to rebuild and strengthen relationships (between the people in the organization and between the people and the organization) and to learn from the experience in order to prepare for the next crisis. In working toward those goals, one of the most effective things leaders can do after the crisis is assure employees that the probability of the same crisis reoccurring is virtually nonexistent. Otherwise, anxiety levels will remain high in the organization and significantly impact morale and productivity. Leaders at all levels should talk to employees and personally share what preventive measures are being taken to avert another crisis. This allows the employees to ask questions, an act that can be therapeutic and calming. Another more formal but particularly effective means of providing such reassurance is through updated and highly publicized company rules and regulations aimed at preventing a similar crisis. These revised rules can outline improved crisis assessment procedures, including early warning and detection, crisis indicators, and improved interpersonal communication methods among leaders and employees in general.

These assurances can be a first step in rebuilding and reviewing the organization's communication strategies. Clear and continuing communication is as essential after a crisis as it is before and during a crisis. Making sure those lines are open after a crisis helps leaders and the organization as a whole learn from their experience and enhance their capability to deal with future crises. It also helps employees connect to the organization, connect to each other, and strengthen the bonds they developed during the crisis.

The idea of rebuilding also extends to operational issues, such as the financial costs of the crisis. The final tally would include such items as cleanup, reconstruction, public relations, recognition and rewards, overtime, and others. Financial compensation may figure into the after-crisis environment and influence the leader's handling of the situation, especially if litigation is part of the picture. (Lawsuits themselves can create an even greater crisis than the one just concluded.)

Review and Revise

A major challenge for the organization's leaders after a crisis is determining all of the causes of the crisis. This is important because if it is not done well or not done at all, the crisis could reoccur. Seldom will a crisis have a single cause. It takes good information, diligent research, and intuitive thinking to reveal all of the causes. All sources of information, no matter how small, should be used in determining the larger causes of the crisis. These sources could include customer feedback, production reports, safety data, employee complaints and suggestions, and others. This process should begin as soon as is practical after the crisis is contained.

In this same vein, the effects of the crisis also require close scrutiny by the organization's leadership. There may be some obvious effects immediately after the crisis, and there is a high probability that other effects will emerge later on. Hidden effects may have even more severe consequences than the primary effects because they may not surface until it's too late to take action—which could bring about another crisis, similar to the aftershock of an earthquake. The determination of all the causes and effects can potentially have a significant impact on the emotions and behaviors of an organization's employees. After a crisis people want to know what happened, why, what it means, and what's being done to make sure it won't happen again. That makes identifying all the causes and effects extremely important to the organization's recovery after the crisis.

A review of how the organization and its leadership handled the crisis should start with a formal or informal assessment of the workforce's emotional state. Some employees may still be in emotional distress, and leaders will want to address those needs. The organization's leadership will want to make sure that the right tools are in place. For example, it might be smart to have counselors available, to encourage workers to take advantage of therapy, and to endorse and underwrite support and discussion groups during work hours. Leaders at all levels of the organization can do their part by walking around and making themselves available to encourage, support, and listen to employees. A personal approach does more than strengthen communication lines—it also builds the relationships that are essential to an organization's surviving the next crisis.

Aside from a review of the organization's emotional state, leaders will want to review how the organization acted and reacted during the crisis. One way to do this is through a process similar to what the army calls its *after action reviews.* During this process, the people most closely involved in the crisis record their impressions and recollections about the organization's response to the crisis—what went well and what could have been done better. Large groups or several small groups can carry out this review. Small groups work better because people in such a setting are more apt to share sensitive information than they would in a larger group. The results of the information-gathering process can be grouped into two categories: validations and lessons learned. Validations reinforce what worked well. Lessons learned break into two camps: those things that did not work well and those things that should have been done but the organization did not know to do.

Organizations and their leadership teams need to be careful not to design or carry out the crisis review as a way to fix blame or to find and punish those guilty of creating the crisis. Rather, the analysis should be focused on answering a single question: What did we learn from the crisis? If needed, there are other formats (formal, organization-based, and even legal outside-the-organization procedures) for determining who, if anyone, is accountable for the crisis. Depending on the nature of the crisis, determining the accountable party or parties and having them appropriately brought to justice is important to the healing of the employees who may see themselves as victims. However, an after action review should focus on learning from the incident and not on determining responsibility, accountability, or guilt. Effective leadership after the crisis will not lose sight of this goal.

The next step is to incorporate the lessons of the crisis review process into the organization's CAP (see Appendix A, pages 75–80). The plan's communication portion should receive special emphasis because of its importance before, during, and after a crisis. Drawing from the lessons learned during the review process, the organization's leadership can update communication tactics ranging from the company's media policy to defining how and to whom employees should report the signs of a potential crisis situation.

The review can also bolster the what-if scenarios that are part of an effective CAP. Further, the crisis review information can be used in writing the final organizational report of the crisis. It's important for leaders to direct the process of updating the response plan and reporting the findings of the review process as soon as possible after the crisis so that key information does not decay or perish.

Beyond the CAP, the organization should expand, eliminate, or change operating procedures, policies, rules, and regulations that were inadequate during the crisis. It should also make adjustments to the assessments or audits created to catch a potential crisis. (Leaders should check to see that fail-safe measures ensure that these audits are actually made and the results reported.) Finally, after the summary report of the crisis has been completed and the response plan has been updated, the organization's leaders can brief employees on the changes and arrange for any needed training. Not only does training communicate changes, but it also meets emotional needs by building employee confidence in the organization's leaders because their crisis-prevention planning is evident.

Communication procedures and organizational policies aren't the only items that might require review and revision following a crisis. Leaders will want to reconsider the organization's vision and values. How did they fare during the crisis? Did they help the organization weather the storm, or did they hinder the organization's response? Was the organization able to live up to its values during the crisis, or did it jettison them in its struggle to survive? These are neither small nor unimportant questions. The leadership may want to realign or redefine the organization's vision and values to make them more potent or relevant to standard operations—and especially to times of crisis. Some existing values may have to be reworded to be stronger, some obsolete values eliminated, and some new values added. Employee safety should be reemphasized. For example, if the values that existed before the crisis were irrelevant or ignored during the crisis, then they should be cut. Otherwise they can become a point of humor among the employees and damage the credibility of the organization's leadership.

Reflect and Renew

In the postcrisis period leaders should also reflect on the deeper meaning of the crisis and how it changed the organization, its culture, and its employees. Some questions for leaders to consider at this stage include the following: What remains the same and what has changed? What changes are complete and what changes are still ongoing? What will never be the same? What are the organizational and cultural adaptations that must be made? Who was most impacted by the event and how are they doing now? William Bridges, the author of *Transitions: Making Sense of Life's Changes*, has written extensively about managing change as a leader. He argues that leaders need to spend time thinking about what they, the organization, and its people have to let go when change happens. That includes changes that a crisis brings. After getting the answers to these questions, leaders can act to address and implement the answers.

Reflecting on the state of relationships is another worthwhile activity after a crisis. Relationships that might have been damaged or stressed during the crisis will need to be rebuilt and strengthened.

Successful efforts to restore relationships throughout the organization highlight forgiveness, provide venues for discussing the issue with all of the people, make it safe to talk about feelings, and take into account the impact that high-stress situations have on relationships.

Within the community of the organization, groups large and small can learn from their experience to prepare for the next crisis. Leaders can have a high emotional impact following a crisis by recognizing and rewarding individuals inside and outside of the organization who made a significant contribution to containing and resolving the crisis. There are several ways in which leaders can make use of or present such recognition. Rewards that can be displayed as a sign of accomplishment and dedication, including but not limited to an appropriate monetary reward, can have a positive, influential impact. Different levels of recognition can reward a variety of contributions, including those who "failed forward" (those people who made honest mistakes and took risks while working hard at resolving the crisis). If there is a question about how many people should be recognized, err on the side of recognizing too many rather than too few contributors. No matter how broad or how meticulously planned for fairness, a small number of employees will no doubt feel slighted. Although those feelings should be acknowledged, they need not be a determining factor in deciding whether or not to create a postcrisis recognition and reward program.

Leaders will also have to turn their attention to the operational needs of the organization after a crisis. For example, some crises may demand significant cleanup that includes recovery, repair, rebuilding, removing, and reorganizing. The organization may need to recruit replacement workers or promote qualified current workers. Leaders should also review human issues. Stress counseling and conflict management are two such areas that might call for vigorous and attentive leadership.

Restore and Reinvigorate

Even if the organization's leaders handled the crisis very well, they and the organization should be prepared for potentially negative consequences. The reputation of the company may be temporarily damaged, lawsuits may result, stock values may dip, crisis-management writers may use the crisis as a negative example in their writings, key leaders and employees may leave, and other problems and challenges may persist after the crisis. For example, a leader may have to spend some time after the crisis helping develop a strategy to restore and improve the organization's reputation if it was damaged during the crisis. An adept and sensitive handling of the crisis can sometimes enhance an organization's reputation, but after a crisis it's obviously too late to get that benefit if the leadership didn't meet the challenge during the crisis. An aggressive postcrisis public relations campaign may help restore an organization's reputation if the crisis wasn't handled as well as it might have been. Such a campaign should focus on organizational stakeholders such as employees, shareholders, the community, and public interest groups. The organization's leadership can't ignore outside scrutiny after the crisis either—the media may be interested in reporting the organization's recovery and repair efforts.

Not all of these actions and considerations are appropriate for every crisis. Leaders will have to determine which ones have application for their organization's situation. But leadership along these lines after a crisis is influential in reducing the emotional impact of the crisis on the employees and strengthening their connection with the organization's leadership. By implementing these and other actions, the leader can restore a sense of security and well-being to people throughout the organization and also to those external stakeholders with a vested interest in the organization's recovery. Beyond the preparation and the handling of the crisis, what is done after the crisis can actually improve employee morale, attitudes, and loyalty, leading to a richer and more effective organization.

To effectively practice crisis leadership, you can't stop at preparation, you can't let yourself be tossed about by the chaos during a crisis, and you can't rest on your laurels when the crisis has passed. To meet the needs of the people in an organization (and crisis comes at one time or another to every organization), leaders must be constantly learning. This is especially crucial during the time after a crisis, when new or validated information can be gathered, analyzed, and applied. Many leaders have significant training, exposure, and experiences, but if they can't gain and apply new information that arises in the period after a crisis, they could miss the entire meaning of the event. In that case, their leadership skills and their organizational preparedness will fall short in the face of any crisis yet to come.

CONCLUSION

In the final analysis, it is all about people.

Because of its intense nature, a crisis triggers emotions, which signal a threat to one or more basic human needs. These needs include such things as safety, security, and self-esteem. When people in an organization feel these needs are threatened, they will behave in ways that ensure their basic needs are met. But because those involved don't always know what to do during a crisis, their behavior may become irrational, unpredictable, and unproductive. Leaders in a crisis situation have to be aware of these connections and respond to the crisis in a way that guides their employees' behaviors toward positive and balanced action, thus ensuring that the organization will weather the crisis and prosper. Simply put, managing and guiding that emotional and behavioral roller coaster is the challenge of leading in a crisis.

No organization or leader is exempt from a crisis. Defined by chaos, confusion, and, in many cases, danger, a crisis is far from business as usual. If not handled correctly, a crisis can destroy an organization and severely limit the career potential of the leaders involved. What such situations require from leaders is competence and a commitment to proven leadership practices.

So what guidelines are there for leaders who want to remain effective during a crisis? As a start, leaders will want to use those skills that deal with the human impact that a crisis exerts on an organization. It's true that leaders have to pay attention to the operational and strategic areas of the organization during a crisis. It's equally important—perhaps even more important given their position—that they pay attention to the people in the organization. Influencing those people to act in responsible and productive ways when the chaos of crisis is all about them is the core of crisis leadership. And that core is comprised chiefly of three components: communication, clarity of vision and values, and a sense of caring in working relationships.

Those three components are essential leadership skills before, during, and after a crisis. By developing strength in them as needed during normal times, responsible leaders can put them into action when a crisis occurs. They will be better able to lead the organization and its people to the other side and even seize opportunity from the dramatic changes that crisis brings. Further, they can minimize the frequency and the severity of a crisis, contain and reduce its effects when it does occur, and learn from it by paying attention to the human side of the crisis.

Before, during, and after a crisis, effective and pervasive communication is vital. Leaders will want to communicate first and foremost with the employees. Second, leaders will want to communicate with external stakeholders such as clients, customers, suppliers, and, if called for, other local community and business leaders. The news media is part of this external stakeholder group, and it's imperative that the leader communicate to the media with the correct facts about the situation, monitor what is reported, and maintain a positive relationship with the media.

One of the principal ideas that effective leaders communicate before, during, and after a crisis is a clarity of vision and values that is reflected in their behavior. A credible set of personal and organizational vision and values and the courage to enact them—in normal times and in times of crisis—provides an anchor and a sense of security for employees. When leaders act in ways that are consistent with those values and that vision, they build trust and ensure mutual respect. They create connections between people in the organization at all levels, and those relationships act as a buffer and reinforcement during a crisis. Employees and others will see the leader as their champion—and someone worth following.

As they examine their own skills at building such connections, leaders can take some direction from simple but effective actions that lay the groundwork for those relationships. For example, leaders can use every opportunity to validate their direct reports and reinforce their self-esteem and self-worth by recognizing, encouraging, and supporting their efforts. In a crisis, leaders who have set a pattern of recognizing performance or have cared enough to respond to the efforts of others can draw upon the resource of a responsive work unit. Even small actions can have a dramatic effect on the self-esteem and self-worth of the people in the organization. Take the time to pat someone on the back, write a note saying "good job," give a certificate of appreciation or commendation, take someone to lunch, or simply recognize an employee in front of colleagues. Other leadership actions that create connections include

- appealing to a sense of loyalty, courage, morality, or other principles that connect the organization's strategy for dealing with the crisis to what is important to people as individuals or as a group
- listening and responding to what your direct reports are telling you
- treating people with sincere consideration and genuine concern and showing it by spending time with them, asking them about the things they are interested in, and considering their hopes and dreams as important as your own
- treating the people you lead with dignity, trust, and respect
- using stories that have a positive application to the situation at hand and using appropriate humor to reduce tension

- accepting others for what they are, without judging
- being truthful and honest, following through with what you say, and avoiding manipulation and deception
- remaining as professionally competent as possible in your area of expertise as well as with specific job responsibilities

Leaders influence others in a crisis very much like they would in normal operations. The primary difference between normal times and crisis situations is that leadership actions are accelerated, amplified, and more visible, and the results of the leadership actions generally have a higher impact when they are taken in the midst of a crisis.

Leaders who want to be as effective as possible during a crisis don't need to start from scratch and learn as they go. They can develop the necessary skills when times are calm and operations are normal. And they can take to heart the lessons and experiences of many organizations (private and public, corporate and not-for-profit, civilian and military) that have studied and practiced the three components of crisis leadership that have proven to be most effective: communication, clarity of vision and values, and caring. With those lessons in mind, leaders can turn the chaos of a crisis into the promise of opportunity and lead people from the turmoil of crisis into the successful perseverance of a resilient, learning organization.

EPILOGUE

(From the Prologue)

... Patton's Third Army did exactly as its leader had promised. His forces were primarily responsible for halting the German attack and also for relieving the encircled American forces at the strategically critical town of Bastogne. Patton achieved this difficult leadership feat (some of his peers had called it impossible) and successfully met this crisis because of carefully honed leadership skills in three areas: communication, clarity of vision and values, and caring.

Patton had few peers as a communicator. During the initial stages of his maneuvers he met face to face with his staff and his subordinate commanders and personally explained the situation and what he expected of them. Patton then visited his units both as they were preparing to move and again later as they were traveling north to attack the Germans. All the while he met with leaders and small groups of soldiers to clarify details of the plan, answer questions, encourage, and prod. He was present, visible, and communicating, as a leader should be in a crisis. Patton used a variety of means to communicate during this period. On Christmas Eve, for example, he issued a small card to each of his soldiers that included his Christmas greeting, his confident assurance that the counterattack would be a success, and a prayer for good weather.

Clarity of vision and values was also a hallmark of Patton's crisis leadership. He had instilled in the soldiers of the Third Army the vision that their sole purpose was to fight and win on the battlefield. He drilled this into his troops at every opportunity so that the vision was clearly understood. He also connected their values—those elements crucial to battlefield success—to the vision. He constantly repeated and reviewed those values (teamwork, mobility, aggressiveness, equipment maintenance, and others) so that when the crisis occurred there was no confusion as to what should be done. That clear vision and associated values provided a solid foundation for his soldiers during the crisis and set a benchmark for personal conduct and attitude.

In the popular imagination, Patton's reputation is of a gruff, boastful, uncaring commander. But imagination isn't always truthful, and it would have been impossible for Patton's troops to achieve what they did during that winter of 1944 in the Ardennes Forest around Bastogne had he not proved to his soldiers that he cared for their well-being. He made sure his soldiers were well equipped for the operation, even going so far as contracting with a Belgian company to make white smocks to camouflage them in the snow-covered Belgian countryside. He also ordered that the soldiers receive a warm Christmas dinner with all the trimmings, and then he visited his units on Christmas Day to ensure his orders had been followed. With this evidence and other proof that their commander cared about them even as he asked them to perform the most difficult task of their lives, the soldiers of the Third Army responded to his leadership and not only survived the crisis but achieved some of the highest historical accolades ever granted to armed forces.

APPENDIX A: The Crisis Action Plan (CAP)

If leaders are to be effective in a crisis, there are a number of things they must do that fall into the category of management. One of those things is the development of a crisis action plan (CAP) that outlines what should be done and by whom when a crisis hits. The leader's management actions are significant because of the potentially high impact these actions will have on the needs, emotions, and behaviors of those being led. Understanding and responding to this impact, both positive and negative, will assist the leader in being more effective in a crisis situation.

Leaders of vision anticipate the possibility of a crisis and know that when a crisis hits it's too late to plan, and, even worse, it's virtually impossible to respond effectively without a plan in place. In addition to directing the creation and use of standard operating procedures, leaders can create a CAP that is ready to implement when a crisis hits. Not only does a CAP prepare an organization for action, but it can also help settle the emotional concerns of many (but not all) employees affected by the crisis.

A prime example of this forward thinking is that of Morgan Stanley, whose offices were located in the World Trade Center. As described by Diane Coutu, Morgan Stanley decided to create a preparedness plan, essentially a CAP, after the 1993 terrorist attack on the Twin Towers. The plan outlined a number of things that included building evacuation routes and alternate places to work when a crisis struck. On September 11, 2001, their crisis action plan was put into effect immediately after the first terrorist plane hit the North Tower. Because of the evacuation triggered by the plan, 2,693 of Stanley's 2,700 employees got out alive. This is a great testimonial to the value of a crisis action plan.

The responsibility for creating a CAP generally falls to the leader in an operational position (such as the chief operations officer, or the vice president for operations). The person in this position can assign the responsibility of creating a CAP to a consultant, or, even better, assign an internal leader or manager to write and staff the plan. The latter approach is more effective because an internal manager has a better knowledge of the organization than an external consultant does. That's likely to mean lower costs, faster completion, more accuracy in detail, and higher credibility with employees. It is important to consider that this approach requires senior leadership in the organization to make sure the manager given the CAP task has the time, resources, and support necessary to carry out the work and create an effective, viable plan.

Another point to consider is that the person selected to draft and coordinate the CAP must, at a minimum, be extremely credible, have highly developed interpersonal skills, be able to effectively communicate both verbally and in writing, and be both intuitive and analytical in temperament. These attributes and skills will help build credibility into the CAP process and into the final plan.

There are several steps to creating a CAP. After the organization has assigned a person to head up the CAP project, that person will need to decide who else should be involved. Organizations that have created and implemented effective CAPs involve leaders at all levels in the planning. The process should certainly involve such positions as department heads and union leaders. It should also include line supervisors—especially those who manage business functions that, if neglected, could trigger a crisis. Broad involvement helps ensure commitment and understanding. Some organizations argue that large-scale involvement of leaders takes too much time and costs too much money. Those costs should be balanced against the cost of not involving all the relevant players. Broader involvement ensures the plan is complete and communicates that the organization takes the planning seriously. Creating a CAP without an enterprise-wide effort and sense of purpose is hardly better than facing a crisis without a plan.

Depending on the type of organization, outsiders may also play a role in the planning process. Leaders from the local community, the government, the news media, and emergency response units such as the police and firefighters can make a big difference in how a crisis plays out in an organization. They can help the organization communicate its response and measure the effectiveness with which it handles the crisis. During a crisis, organizations need many allies and few adversaries. Involving leaders from external groups in the crisis planning process goes a long way in putting them on your side.

A useful strategy in devising a CAP is to assign someone who is highly credible and has outstanding critical-thinking skills as devil's advocate. This person's role is to challenge and question everything in the plan (for example, Why is this item in the plan? Is this section complete? What could be added to the plan? Is the plan clear and specific enough for those who would have to implement it? Who will install the phones and computers in the command center? When during the crisis will that happen? Is the plan realistic, or can it be put into effect?). The goal of this argumentative preview is to make the CAP practical, complete, and viable.

The next step in developing a CAP is deciding what goes into it. The CAP is not the place for abstract theories or philosophical hypotheses. It should be very practical and functional, with clear guidelines outlining what should be done and when. For example, the plan could state "When X occurs, the person in this position should . . . ." Optimally, the CAP should also define relationships and responsibilities and provide the authority for the various actions that will need to be taken when a crisis occurs and the plan is implemented. If the CAP is detailed and practical, less time will be wasted resolving such issues during the crisis.

Communication processes are important to every CAP. Well-defined and easily understood reporting procedures can avert a crisis in the first place and reduce the impact of the crisis when it occurs. What is to be reported, when, to whom (the reporting chain), with what sense of urgency, and in what format are all crucial elements of crisis planning. Any additional communications equipment needed for the crisis should be listed. This could include anything from a bullhorn and portable radios to an information hot line or a toll-free number. Your organization may also need a bank of computers for use in its command center.

Communication channels must also be planned for key stakeholders outside of the organization. These would include employee families, the news media, stockholders, community and government officials, customers, and suppliers. The CAP should describe exactly how and by what means they will be informed of the crisis and kept up to date. It can be helpful to draft some general language into the plan that can be used to reassure everyone when the crisis occurs.

How the CAP itself is to be communicated to the organization's workforce is also an important factor. Certainly it should become part of the organization's overall training program. One difficult leadership challenge in preparing for a crisis is convincing employees that a crisis could actually occur and that training for such a contingency isn't a waste of time. There are several steps a leader can take to communicate the CAP across the organization.

First, brief leaders at all levels, and then brief employees, on the contents of the plan. Second, plan exercises for implementing parts of the CAP on a regular basis (annually will do). Leaders can schedule such activities as drills and rehearsals. A worst-case scenario exercise might involve, for example, the simulated failure of the organization's most reliable and mission-critical systems and equipment. Internal communication—the reporting and passing of critical information—should be a key part of these exercises. After the exercise, conduct a review to capture lessons and to highlight mistakes, and then use that information to refine the CAP.

An organization can't cover all possible contingencies. Common crises such as fire and natural disasters should definitely be considered. The checklist on page 80 (which is by no means comprehensive) is a starting point for developing a plan that accounts for almost any potential crisis. An organization can set the tone for how it will deal with crisis and emergency situations by using this list and other sources (books and articles, consultants who specialize in crisis management, and leaders outside the organization who either have been involved in a crisis or who have extensive experience in crisis contingency planning).

Crisis Action Plan Checklist

❏ Define what constitutes a crisis for your organization and what does not.

❏ Develop and implement risk identification and assessment procedures.

❏ Define events and indicators that show a crisis is imminent.

❏ Define the immediate actions to be taken when a crisis occurs.

❏ Select who activates the CAP and how it occurs (that is, what is the first step?).

❏ Develop a detailed internal and external communication plan with specific reporting and notification responsibilities.

❏ Discuss the organization's general policy regarding the media.

❏ Define responsibilities for leaders and key employees during the crisis (for example, who staffs the command center, and who leads the crisis response teams).

❏ Specify locations and equipment for the command center, the crisis response teams, the media briefing area (if needed), and other operations.

❏ Specify locations for any special equipment and resources to be used during the crisis and specify the people who have access to them.

❏ Develop detailed evacuation procedures with safety as a prime consideration.

❏ Create a precrisis checklist for all departments or units to measure compliance, levels of commitment to the process, and overall preparation.

APPENDIX B: What Leaders Can Do to Take Care of Themselves During a Crisis

During a crisis leaders are often concerned with the emotional turmoil of their direct reports and others in the organization. That's the way it should be, as the human impact of a crisis has a good deal to do with whether or not an organization can seize opportunity from the turbulence it finds itself in, or if it can even survive the crisis at all. Leaders are also absorbed with managerial tasks designed to keep the organization running on a functional level. Both of these leadership tasks are important, but it's equally important for leaders to take care of themselves during a crisis. They should be aware of their own emotional turmoil, its effect on their behavior, and its influence on their leadership abilities. This list of ideas, practices, and reminders can help leaders keep the perspective they need to bring their people and their organization through a crisis.

- Think "today." Take the crisis one day at a time.
- Seek more social support from work relationships, personal relationships, and friendships.
- Talk to people you trust about how you are feeling.
- Write letters, cards, and notes to people to express your thoughts about the situation.
- Avoid negative people.
- Spend more time with your pets.
- Keep a journal; write down what you are thinking, your impressions, and your reactions.
- Practice relaxation techniques such as meditation and deep breathing.
- Practice spiritual exercises as they fit your individual beliefs.
- Exercise, even if it's just walking.
- Eat healthier foods both at meals and for snacks.

- Reduce your intake of coffee and other products containing caffeine.
- Reduce or temporarily eliminate the use of alcoholic beverages.
- Get more sleep, including naps.
- Laugh, tell jokes, or rent a comedy video.
- Take five-minute private breaks.
- Cry if you have to.
- Listen to soft music. Listen to loud music. Dance and sing to both.
- Read a favorite book or story.
- Spend time doing a favorite activity or hobby.
- Write a short story or a poem. Draw a picture.
- Get a massage.
- Light a candle. Light many candles.
- Now, more than ever, do all things in moderation.
- Use positive self-talk. Avoid negative thoughts and negative talk.
- Constantly think positive thoughts and that you can do it.
- Keep meetings short or "on the hoof," where everyone stands.
- Be more assertive. Say "no" more often.
- Be more conscious about managing your time and priorities.
- Concentrate on only major issues. Skip secondary tasks.
- Make plans to travel and to do other fun things after the crisis has passed.
- In your mind, take a three- to five-minute trip to the beach, the mountains, or wherever you like to go to get away from it all.
- Concentrate on the greater vision you have of yourself, both personally and professionally. Think about where you will be and what you will be doing a year from now.
- Stop and realize that you are alive and that much good will come out of the crisis.

SUGGESTED READINGS

Albrecht, S. W. (1996). *Crisis management for corporate self-defense: How to protect your organization in a crisis . . . how to stop a crisis before it starts.* New York: AMACOM.

Ambrose, S. E. (2001). *Band of brothers.* New York: Simon & Schuster.

Andriole, S. J. (Ed.). (1985). *Corporate crisis management.* Princeton, NJ: Petrocelli Books.

Barton, L. (1992). *Crisis in organizations: Managing and communicating in the heat of chaos.* Cincinnati: South-Western Publishing.

Bridges, W. (1980). *Transitions: Making sense of life's changes.* Reading, MA: Addison-Wesley.

Browning, H., & Van Velsor, E. (1999). *Three keys to development: Defining and meeting your leadership challenges.* Greensboro, NC: Center for Creative Leadership.

Cartwright, T. (2003). *Managing conflict with peers.* Greensboro, NC: Center for Creative Leadership.

Cohn, R. (2000). *The PR crisis bible: How to take charge of the media when all hell breaks loose.* New York: St. Martin's Press.

Coutu, D. (2002). How resilience works. *Harvard Business Review, 80*(5), 46–55.

Davis, W. (1987). *The innovators.* New York: AMACOM.

Doughtery, D. (1992). *Crisis communications: What every executive needs to know.* New York: Walker.

Fink, S. (2000). *Crisis management: Planning for the inevitable.* New York: AMACOM.

Giglotti, R. J., & Jason, R. C. (1991). *Emergency planning for maximum protection.* Boston: Butterworth-Heinemann.

Giuliani, R. W. (2002). *Leadership.* Waterville, ME: Thorndike Press.

Goleman, D. (1995). *Emotional intelligence. New York: Bantam Books.*

Harvard business review on crisis management. (2000). Boston: Harvard Business School Press.

Heath, R. (1998). *Crisis management for managers and executives: Business crises, the definitive handbook to reduction, readiness, response, and recovery.* London: Financial Times/Pitman Publishing.

Kennett, L. B. (1987). *G.I.: The American soldier in World War II.* New York: Scribner.

Klann, G. (1999). *A model for developing ground combat leaders.* Unpublished doctoral dissertation. Free University of Brussels, Brussels, Belgium.

Knud, J. (Ed.). (1997). *European approaches to crisis management.* Hague, Netherlands: Kluwer Law International.

Lagadec, P. (1993). *Preventing chaos in a crisis: Strategies for prevention, control, and damage limitation.* New York: McGraw-Hill.

Lerbinger, O. (1986). *Managing corporate crises: Strategies for executives.* Boston: Barrington Press.

Lombardo, M., & Eichinger, R. W. (1989). *Preventing derailment: What to do before it's too late.* Greensboro, NC: Center for Creative Leadership.

Marshall, S. L. A. (2000). *Men against fire: The problem of battle command.* Norman: University of Oklahoma Press.

Maslow, A. (1970). *Motivation and personality* (3rd ed.). New York: Harper & Row.

Meyers, G. C., & Holusha, J. (1986). *When it hits the fan: Managing the nine crises of business.* Boston: Houghton Mifflin.

Mitroff, I. I., & Anagnos, G. (2001). *Managing crises before they happen: What every executive and manager needs to know about crises management.* New York: AMACOM.

Mitroff, I. I., & Pearson, C. M. (1993). *Crisis management: A diagnostic guide for improving your organization's crisis preparedness.* San Francisco: Jossey-Bass.

Mitroff, I. I., Pearson, C. M., & Harrington, L. K. (1996). *The essential guide to managing corporate crises: A step-by-step handbook for surviving major catastrophes.* New York: Oxford University Press.

Pinsdorf, M. K. (1987). *Communicating when your company is under siege: Surviving public crisis.* Lexington, MA: Lexington Books.

Popejoy, B., & McManigle, B. J. (2002). *Managing conflict with direct reports.* Greensboro, NC: Center for Creative Leadership.

Pulley, M. L., & Wakefield, M. (2001). *Building resiliency: How to thrive in times of change.* Greensboro, NC: Center for Creative

Leadership.

Register, M., & Larkin, J. (1998). *Risk issues and crisis management: A casebook of best practices.* London: Kogan Page.

Sharpe, D., & Johnson, E. (2002). *Managing conflict with your boss.* Greensboro, NC: Center for Creative Leadership.

Silva, M., & McGann, T. (1995). *Overdrive: Managing in crisis-filled times.* New York: John Wiley & Sons.

Stouffer, S. (Ed.). (1949). *The American soldier: Combat and its aftermath* (Vols. 1–5). Princeton, NJ: Princeton University Press.

Weitzel, S. (2000). *Feedback that works: How to build and deliver your message.* Greensboro, NC: Center for Creative Leadership.

Yukl, G. (1989). *Leadership in organizations.* Englewood Cliffs, NJ: Prentice Hall.

Ordering Information

To get more information, to order other CCL Press publications, or to find out about bulk-order discounts, please contact us by phone at 336-545-2810 or visit our online bookstore at **www.ccl.org/publications**.